For K[illegible]

God's Best to you!

[illegible]

2/8/03

Spiritual Chocolate

Spiritual Chocolate

Inspirational Delights for the Heart

Dr. Glenn Mollette

Inspiration
Newburgh, Indiana
A Division of GMA Publishing

Email address GMAPublishing@aol.com

Telephone Orders 1 800-810-2500

ISBN: 0-9704650-2-5

Cover by Kim Schum

Printed in the United States of America

Acknowledgements

Thanks for pausing here as I acknowledge the support and help I've received from so many inspirational and delightful people:

To Karen, my wife of over 25 years, and the love of my life, who has always found a way to say something good about my sermons—Your sheer courage in facing multiple sclerosis has changed my life and ministry.

To Jared and Zachary, two wonderful children that I love and adore—You two guys will always be my best friends.

To Mom and Dad, Eula and Walter—You encouraged me in my life, education and ministry.

To the churches and people along the way who have inspired and blessed my life—Thank you for the great opportunities.

To Gateway Baptist Church—A special thanks for your incredible support and love, allowing me the freedom to care for Karen, write messages I feel enthusiastic about preaching, and giving me the opportunity to have a great eight-year ministry.

Cover Interpretation

Spiritual Chocolate is about the good, sweet and delightful life that God has for us in Christ. While much of life has its valley's and trials, God provides a newness of life that nothing in the world can give to us. This life is one of hope, power, stamina, peace and the ability to soar even when life's conditions seem unfavorable for flying. The very best treasures in life come directly from the heart of God. He loves us. This chocolate is good for you! Open up the lid to this box and savor God's marvelous inspirational delights!

Contents

CHAPTER ONE

Spiritual Chocolate
Inspirational Delights for the Heart

Valentine's day is a big day for chocolate. I'm not sure what day is not a big day for chocolate. It flows freely almost year around; and Christmas time finds chocolate everywhere. Candy stores that make fine chocolate seem to always be in season. When is chocolate ever out of season?

We know that too much is not good for our waistlines, our teeth, our complexion or our health in general. But some leading authorities are saying that dark chocolate occasionally is good for us. I'm on their side. Of course this is the same people that are saying red wine on occasion is good for us. One researcher says it's not the alcohol but the red pigment that is favorable to our health. Apparently it's the same ingredient that you might find in strawberries or grape juice. Anyhow, you may be a diabetic and therefore you have had to renounce chocolate. And I suppose if you go without any for a long enough period you just lose your taste for it.

But I say here . . . let's open this box of chocolate. Everybody smiles. Oh there will be some crabby person that's on a diet that will frown. But by and large you open a box of chocolate and there is always an aura of delight. So here take one. Forest Gump reminded us, "You never know what you're going to get." So I have for you a box of only the finest chocolate. Not one selection of this fine candy is unsavory to your palate. Every piece will bring a smile to your face and will cause you to say *mmmm*. I have to caution you that once you start you won't want to stop. Are you that way with chocolate sometimes? One piece leads to another? And then you eat the whole box? This box of chocolates I have for you is the specialty of the house and I think if you take one you will want some more. But that's okay, because this chocolate is fat free, sugar free and has no carbohydrates and is the best you will ever taste.

Psalm 34:8, "Taste and see that the Lord is good; blessed is the man who takes refuge in him." Psalm 119:103, "How sweet are your words to my taste, sweeter than honey to my mouth!" The word of God is sweet. The Lord is Good. Whether we are reading the Sermon on the Mount or the book of Psalms, the Bible is filled with delectable words that are a delight to the taste buds of our hearts.

Psalm 37:1–9 is one of many such passages. It is a passage that is sweet to our soul. Let's see what we have here. Let's open this particular box and we find three specialties. Here take one! Enjoy a fret not. Try it. Have you ever had a fret not? Come on and try it and see what it does for you. It might give you a charge. It will take that old frown off your face and give you smile. This psalm says, "Do not fret because of evil men or be envious of those who do wrong; for like the grass they will soon wither, like green plants they will soon die away." Verse eight says, "Do not fret—it leads only to evil."

Fretting is being anxious. Fretting is wringing our hands. Fretting is worrying. Fretting is going on and on and on. The Bible says, "Don't fret." Time and again Jesus taught us in Matthew chapter six to fret not. "Who of you by worrying can add a single hour to his life?" (Matthew 6:27) The truth of the matter is you are likely to shorten your life by worrying and fretting. Take one. Try a fret not.

Next, delight in a fear not. Do you understand fear? The doctor says, "It's cancer." Does that do anything to you? Not until it comes close to home.

Big layoff at work coming and a hundred people are going to be involved. Does that do anything to you? It's 2:00 in the morning and your child hasn't come home. You or somebody you love is pregnant . . . but the doctor says, "There's something wrong with the baby." Most all of us have had or do have our fears. You know what fear is? We all at some point experience cold, clammy, sweaty, bone chilling fear.

But David said in Psalm 34:4, "I sought the Lord, and he answered me; he delivered me from all my fears." Is that possible? What do you fear? What is it that you fear that God cannot see you through? I felt like I understood multiple sclerosis enough eleven years ago to know where it might take my family and I was right. I had seen MS as a teenager so I had an understanding of it. And because I knew what the disease could do, that made me fearful for my wife Karen, and all of us. We have fought it tooth and toenail every inch of the way. Friend, when it comes to our bodies we are not invincible. Somewhere along the way we are going to lose the battle with disease. But that doesn't mean that we just give up and roll over. No! We seek the Lord like David did and He helps us to work through it. In the midst of the battles of life, He gives us peace that passes understanding.

What kind of fear do you have? Spouse fears? Children fears? Aged parents? Job stress? People in general? Health fears? Financial worries?

> *In the midst of the battles of life, He gives us peace that passes understanding.*

David said, "I sought the Lord." Have you really honestly tried bringing God into the matter? Have you looked to Him? Delight yourself in a fear not. Take one. Don't live every day in clammy, cold, icy fear.

In Isaiah chapter 41, God is the great helper of Israel. And indeed He was. He said in verse 13, "'For I am the Lord, your God, who takes hold of your right hand and says to you, Do not fear; I will help you. Do not be afraid . . . for I myself will help you,' declares the Lord." Will you claim this verse for your life?

Now, revive yourself with a faint not. Have you ever fainted? Psalm 37:7 tells us to wait patiently before the Lord. In other words don't faint. Don't quit. Don't give up.

What revives you? Is it a good night's sleep? Or, is it a good meal? Is it a good hour of exercise? Is it being with somebody that you think is just wonderful? Or is it Advil and Ben Gay? Whatever works is what we normally pursue.

But Isaiah says in chapter 40:29-31, "He gives strength to the weary and increases the power of the weak. Even youths grow tired and weary, and young men stumble and fall; but those who hope in the Lord will renew their strength. They will soar on wings like eagles; they will run and not grow weary, they will walk and not be faint."

Do you need a faint not? Are you about to faint in life? Are you fainting in the Lord's work? Are you fainting in your relationship with Jesus Christ? He will give you strength. He will enable you to soar on wings like eagles—keep walking and not be faint.

Notice the key words in Psalm 37:3, "Trust in the Lord and do good." Noah trusted God and worked on a boat for a hundred years. Don't you think he ever got sick and tired of it? Surely he did. But it paid off. He saved himself, his family and two animals of every kind the Bible says. Every day we find him trusting God and trying to do the right thing. It paid off. You can't go wrong when you are faithful to God and trying to do what is right.

Job had every mortal excuse to curse God and turn against him, but he said, "Though he slay me, yet will I hope in him," Job 13:15.

"Delight yourself in the Lord and he will give you the desires of your heart," Psalm 37: 4. What do you want? Answer that question? What would it take to make you happy? How are you going to have it? Are you going to obtain it through hook, crook, deceit, conniving, or theft? Whenever you go through unlawful means to obtain the desires of your heart you are giving a part of yourself away. You are destroying a part of yourself.

I'm not sure what all you and I can have. But He has promised us the key essentials of life. He has promised in Matthew chapter six that He will take care of us. He has promised us in Galatians chapter five that He will give us love, peace, joy, patience, kindness and control in our lives.

That's what so many people are looking for. You want love. I hear that all the time. "I just want somebody to love. I want somebody to love me." God has promised us He will meet that need in our lives. "I am restless." "My life is in a million pieces." There is peace in the Lord, dear friend. Jesus said, "Come to me, all you who are weary and are burdened and I will give you rest," (Matthew 11:28).

Are you weary in your heart? Are you weary in your spirit? Are you facing trials of every kind? Delight yourself in the Lord and He will give you the desires of your heart. Take all three here. This psalm teaches us to fret not, fear not and faint not.

Commit Your Way to the Lord

Number one is here again—trust Him. Do you remember ever hearing this song, "Trust and obey for there is no other way to be happy in Jesus than to trust and obey."[1]

Are you happy in Jesus? Have you ever been around a miserable person? In the New Testament we have the story of Judas who became very unhappy with his life. He had been on Jesus' side for three years . . . or at least it appeared that he was and then he changes. His true colors come out. He betrays the Lord for almost nothing. And he is so miserable with his life he kills himself.

Pilate was in such a fix about what to do with Jesus. He tried washing his hands of Christ but that didn't help. And Peter—he became fickle in Christ's greatest hour of need. And it broke his heart when he remembered that Jesus said, "This very night, before the rooster crows, you will disown me three times," (Matthew 26:34). The most miserable person in the world is a Christian who has lost his way. Paul wrote about "Demas, because he

---

[1] *Trust and Obey*, The Baptist Hymnal, (Nashville: Convention Press, 1991) 447.

loved this world, has deserted me and has gone to Thessalonica," (2 Timothy 4:10).

Are you in limbo in your life? Is there an area where you need to make a commitment? There is something about committing yourself and saying, "I'm going to do it!" This is the way I am going with my life. I'm going to make it. You see when you decide within your spirit I'm going to go forward with this . . . then your spirit is revived. There is an energy rush. Remember we talked about a faint not? Faint not comes when we decide on our way . . . our direction in life!

There is something about committing yourself and saying, "I'm going to do it!"

Be Still Before the Lord

Be still before the Lord. This is tough. We don't have that kind of generation here in our country. This is so foreign to us because we want everything so fast. Fast money. Fast education. Fast success. Fast food. Sitting down and being still is tough for some of us.

But we know if we are going to have anything happen positively in our relationships, we have to have some quiet time. We have to be still . . . and listen.

Moses pulled off his sandals and got real quiet before a burning bush in the book of Exodus. Things got quiet . . . and God had a word for him.

Some of the greatest moments in the Bible happened when things got still. When Jesus started washing the disciples feet there was a hush that fell over that room. They couldn't believe at first what Jesus was doing.

The Garden of Gethsemane was a still place . . . disciples sleeping, Jesus agonizing with the Father.

When Jesus was preaching the Sermon on the Mount it had to be quiet or nobody could have heard what this great teacher was saying.

On the cross Jesus cried *It Is Finished* and then there was an eerie quietness and darkness that surrounded the cross.

Daniel is often pictured in the lion's den facing a ray of light with his hands tied . . . as though he is being very still before the Lord.

Most of the time instead of fretting and gnawing our guts out, we need to be still and see what God is doing. And if God is at work . . . then join in.

Most of the time instead of fretting and gnawing our guts out, we need to be still and see what God is doing.

Wait Patiently

Joseph waited in prison for 13 years. It looked like he would never see the light of day. Then one day he was freed and he went on to be greatly used of God.

I watched Jim Bakker and his new wife, and Tammy Faye and their son Jay on Larry King. Jim Bakker had a one day 15 minute sexual encounter with Jessica Hahn back in the late eighties. Then he was involved in a land deal that went sour. Apartments and time-shares were oversold. And so it seemed like everybody that had ever wanted an opportunity to get a well-known Christian had their opportunity to pour it on Jim Bakker. By his own admission in his own book he writes, "I was wrong. I made some mistakes."

But my point is Jim Bakker came back to be used of God in Southern California. He has a beautiful wife. Their son Jay, who suffered so much through all that the family endured, has written a great book. And God seems to be at work in these people's lives. I say, to God be the glory that He can take broken vessels, remold them . . . reshape them . . . and use them again.

Isaiah 40:31, "But those who hope in the Lord will renew their strength." I say, be patient. Are you still alive? Don't give up on God. Don't give up on yourself. Sometimes you feel as though you are never going to see the sunshine again. But be patient the Bible says, and don't faint.

Refrain From Anger

Anger and a box of chocolate do not go together. Have you ever given someone a box of chocolate in anger? Of course not. "Do not fret" the scripture says, it leads only to evil. Here is another fret not.

Are you angry? Are you mad at somebody? There is never any delight when we allow ourselves to seethe with anger.

The Bible says, "Be delighted." Delight yourself in the Lord. The heart is inspired and delighted when we bask in the spiritual good things God has provided. We have talked about taking a fret not, a fear not, a faint not . . . but to have these enjoyable delights, we have to take the one who is the source of spiritual delight. His name is Jesus. He is our source of delight. He brought delight to every home. Wherever He was, the occasion was one of delight.

Mary and Martha were miserable because Lazarus had died. Jesus turned it all around.

Jairus was a broken man because of his little girl's illness. Jesus turned the situation around.

A widow stood in the street and wept over her dead son. Jesus turned the funeral into a party.

When a wedding almost went south, Jesus brought delight to the party.

When Zacchaeus was saved, Jesus showed him and his friends what a real party was all about.

When disciples hung their heads with heavy hearts walking to a little getaway village called Emmaus, Jesus joined them after his resurrection. As He talked with them their hearts burned within them. And they did a seven-mile run back to Jerusalem to tell everybody with delight that Jesus was alive and that He really had done what He said He would do.

The Bible says, "Delight yourself in the Lord and he will give you the desires of your heart." Delight yourself in Him!

CHAPTER ONE
REFLECTION AND MEDITATION

1. What is fretting?

2. What should we do with our fears?

3. When we are about to faint, Isaiah 40:29-31 has a message of inspiration.

4. According to Matthew chapter six, what has God promised to do?

5. Key challenges from this chapter:

    a. Commit your way to the Lord.
    b. Be still before Him.
    c. Wait patiently.
    d. Refrain from anger.

CHAPTER TWO

What Do You Really Want?

Sometimes testimonies come from what we feel—or how we feel. The tone of someone's testimony often hinge's on the tenor of their experience—what they have been through.

Here is someone that has been in the gutter of life, drunk, drug crazed for several years and then comes to know Jesus Christ. His testimony will be that of God rescuing him from drugs and alcohol and giving him a clean and sober life—helping him to live in his right mind.

Or here is someone that commits a terrible crime and he is sentenced to prison. But in the prison house he realizes how awful life has become and how lost he is without Christ and he takes hold of His love and God then gives him new life in Christ.

Or here is someone who likely has it all. She may have achieved about all that life can give. She has established a wonderful career, has a beautiful family, money is not a problem, and health is good. But yet within her heart she comes to realize that everything that can be had in this life does not fill the deepest need of the heart and only that need can ever truly be met by knowing God's love in His Son, Jesus Christ. And so she says I have had it all, but I have come to realize that there was much more in knowing Christ.

Our testimonies are often based on what God has proven to us. Maybe there was a time in your life when you didn't know how you were going to make it but God somehow saw you through and you knew it was only by God's grace that you were seen through. So you say, I believe in God because I know if it had not been for Him, there is no way I would have come through that time in my life.

I gave thanks when my Father had an aneurysm removed from his aorta. They cut it out, inserted a plastic tube and he was good to go. When they first found this aneurysm the doctor said it was small. When the surgeon greeted us after the surgery was performed in Lexington, Kentucky, he showed us his fist and said that the aneurysm was the size of his fist. We knew God had been merciful because it sounded like that aneurysm had been removed in just the nick of time. And so from that experience we can give thanks and say God has been gracious and good and He has helped us.

Chances are that a part of your testimony as a Christian is: "Yes, from experience I know that God is real. There was a time when God provided a job or when God saw me through a hard time or when God gave me an open door or when there was some kind of break-through in my life." And so we give testimony based on that experience.

We give testimony based on what we feel and on what we have experienced. But we also give testimony based on God's word.

Throughout the scriptures we have countless words of hope, encouragement and direction. There are times when we don't know what to do but we look to God's word; and His word instructs us.

"Your word *is* a lamp to my feet, and a light for my path." (Psalms 119:105).

"I have hidden your word in my heart that I might not sin against you." (Psalms 119:11)

There are times when we don't know what to do but we look to God's word; and His word instructs us.

Another is, "Faith cometh by hearing, and hearing by the word of God." (Romans 10:17)

And so there are days when we say . . . Well . . . I don't know how to feel . . . and I don't have any touchstones or experiences in life to base this on or to relate this to but God's word says . . . He will be with us always. And, He is with us in the valley.

His word says, "The one who is in you is greater than the one who is in the world," (1 John 4:4). We go to God's word and we see how He took care of those who loved Him.

Hebrews 11:1 and 3, "Now faith is being sure of what we hope for and certain of what we do not see. This is what the ancients were commended for. By faith we understand that the universe was formed at God's command, so that what is seen was not made out of what was visible." And then we see a hall of fame listing of Biblical characters that were people who lived their lives based on the word they had from God.

Noah built his ark based on the word he had from God. Abraham made his decisions based on the word that he had from God. Moses led the people of God based on the word he had from God.

When we make any decision based on what we have read in God's word it will then render feelings and experiences. We will say, "I decided I was going to do and try what the Bible said to do and this has been my experience. This has been the result of believing God and trusting Him.

In the Old Testament book of Malachi we read about God challenging His people to return to Him and trust Him and put Him first in the way they live and in their giving and then He gives them this word, Malachi 3:9 says, "Test me in this," says the Lord Almighty, "and see if I will not throw open the floodgates of heaven and pour out so much blessing that you will not have room enough for it."

Have you tried loving God supremely and putting God first in your life? Have you experienced the truth of Malachi 3:9? I don't believe I have met anyone who has ever said, "I gave my best to God and the promises of Malachi 3:9 are not true."

I think a part of our testimony is based on the fact that yes we have tried God's word and believed His word. And there have been times when He has opened the floodgates of heaven and poured out so much blessing that there has not been enough room to receive it.

Therefore the *desire of my heart . . . what I really want* is as follows:

Love God More

Loving God more is a good thing to do. I can't figure out why anybody would not want to. Can you? Why would anybody not want to love God?

Jude 21, "Keep yourselves in the Love of God."

Psalm 37:4, "Delight yourself in the Lord and he will give you the desires of your heart."

> *Why would you want anything less than God's very best that He has for you?*

I want to say from feeling, but also from proven experience that Psalm 37:4 is true. In so many ways the Lord has given me everything I need. He wants to do this. He wants to do it for you! Why would you want anything less than God's very best that He has for you?

I have His presence. I have His word to instruct me. I have this beautiful world that He has created for my service to Him and for my enjoyment.

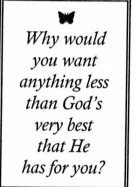

I live in a country where there are so many vast opportunities and freedom to have such a great life. I have a beautiful wife and wonderful children, and a great church family. My parents and brothers and sisters are all Christians. I am very grateful. And so I want to love God more.

I want to love Him because He has been willing to love me in spite of all my sins and failures and shortcomings. And I figure if God can love a sinner like me and give me eternal life then He really must be an incredible God.

John 3:16 proves this over and over again. "For God so loved the world that he gave his one and only Son, that whoever believes in him shall not perish but have eternal life."

Love My Wife More

My wife and I will have been married at this writing over 25 years. I don't know how we've made it 25 years except I guess my wife has been really good at putting up with me.

The Bible tells us as husbands to love our wives. But I don't think we need a lot of scripture to know that's what we as men are supposed to do. We know from first hand experience that life and home and even our relationship with God are best when we are truly loving our wives.

Illness is not easy. Caring for somebody even though they are as beautiful as my wife is not an easy thing. But there is a different kind of blessing in care giving. When you become the caregiver to your wife or husband you have the opportunity then to prove that you love them.

One of the biggest weddings ever to have happened in Kentucky happened in the fall of 2000. The state's Lt. Governor married Miss America in Louisville. The wedding, someone estimated, cost a lot of money. He was one of Kentucky's premier eligible bachelors . . . rich, smart and a political leader. She was the most recent Miss America . . . a good-looking woman.

So you have Kentucky's number one eligible bachelor, marrying Kentucky's highest profile single woman. And at a time like that in life it's real easy to say, "I'll love you for richer or poorer." What if they really became dirt poor, would they still love each other? When prince Charles and Lady Diana got married and they said we are going to love each other for richer or poorer, I thought "fat chance of the latter."

Or what about in sickness and in health? Can you love your wife if she got sick and you could never again have sex with her . . . for years? Ma'am could you be faithful to your husband if three or four times a day you had to change his diaper and give him a bath . . . and feed him like a baby?

That day is likely coming for you unless you die suddenly. Everybody gets to go through care giving at some point in life. Either someday you will be caring for your spouse as an invalid or your spouse will be doing it for you. And, you won't really feel like doing it.

But the Bible says, "Husbands love your wives just as Christ loved the church and gave himself up for her," (Ephesians 5:25). There is a part of marriage where we love each other as Christ loves us. And Christ loves us sacrificially. Jesus went to the cross for our sins and shortcomings and died for us.

Sometimes in the marriage relationship we die a little for the other person. Sometimes we do it a lot.

I give thanks for my wife. I praise God for her. I hate the disease that has plagued her body—multiple sclerosis. But I praise God for what He has taught and is teaching me.

Love My Children More

My dad called my house Thursday afternoon before he went to the hospital for surgery because I'm sure he feared maybe he wouldn't have the chance again down here.

Now my father and I have never had the kind of relationship of playing ball or fishing together because I know that when you drive an hour one way to get to work . . . spend all day in a coal mine and then drive an hour back home . . . you're beat. I understood that as a kid. But he was always there when I needed him.

When I was 15 years old my first cousin and I wrecked my dad's truck one night while my mom and dad were away at church. We wrecked it right in front of some little country church that was having this big revival meeting. There must have been 300 people in that church. I just knew my dad would kill me, but he let me live.

Can you imagine? That would be like my son Zach who is now 15 doing something like that. But throughout life whenever I was down, my dad was there. God is like that. 2 Thessalonians 2:16, "Our Father, who loved us and by his grace gave us eternal encouragement and good hope."

I need God's love and our children need that, too. I want to love Jared and Zachary like that.

Love People More

I suppose loving people should be automatic. But we know loving others is not always so easy. Sometimes it takes work. The average person in the world knows how good it is to have someone care about them and to be loved.

Jesus taught us "Love the Lord your God with all your heart and with all your soul and with all your mind and with all your strength." (Mark 12:30)

My neighbor down the street and I did not get off to a good relationship when he got me out of the shower one day to fuss to me about the behavior of my teenage boys. I stood in the doorway—dripping wet as he espoused to me his dislike about the way my boys had been acting when they went by his house. I assured him I would discuss the matter with my kids and would work to correct any problems. For almost two years there was coldness between he and I that was not getting resolved.

And I wasn't doing any more about resolving it than he was.

One big snowy day I came home and saw a man shoveling snow out of my driveway. I couldn't believe it. It was my neighbor from down the street. I was stunned. "This can't be true," I thought. "This guy is too big of a jerk to do anything like this." However, it was true and when I got out of my car to greet him he said, "I consider myself a Christian and I've thought more than once, I wonder what that guy down the street thinks about me." He continued to shovel snow. I took him a box of candy. Hopefully we can be good neighbors.

So much of our life hinges on our friendships and relationships with others.

An old saying is, to live up above with those that we love, oh that will be glory. But to dwell here below with those that we know, that's another story.

So much of our life hinges on our friendships and relationships with others. Is there someone that you need to call, send an email or card, or go visit?

Our wants may not really be the extravagant possessions of life. But our greatest desires may be most greatly satisfied by our love for God, spouse or other loved ones, children and people.

CHAPTER TWO
REFLECTION AND MEDITATION

1. Our testimonies are often based on what God has proven to us. What has God proven to you?

2. Our testimony foremost is based on God's word. There are times when we don't know what to do but we look to God's word; and His word instructs us. What are some of His promises?

3. Based on how God has proven Himself to you; and foremost on His word, the Bible, what is the desire of your heart?

CHAPTER THREE

How To Use Words Effectively

How do you express yourself? How do you utilize the tone in your voice? How do you communicate with body language? We communicate in some way all the time. We are constantly sending signals by our facial expressions countenance and posture. Sometimes people can be overly demonstrative in the way they communicate. They stomp their feet or they raise their voice or get too close to someone's face. Most of us have seen this kind of behavior.

The eyes of the nation were upon our state when the coach of Indiana University was terminated. We heard about the termination of Indiana University Coach Bobby Knight on a Sunday afternoon. Many in our area watched him on ESPN television and then he was carried by CNN television live as he spoke to the student body.

I was very sad by the whole ordeal for Indiana University, Bobby Knight, and the game of Basketball.

The basketball record of Bobby Knight is incredible. The fact that his program in 29 years never received a violation from the NCAA is almost unbelievable. Dean Smith, former coach of North Carolina was quoted on ESPN television as saying, "Every time the media shows Knight throwing that chair across the court, he wishes they would also show his record with the NCAA. Here is a guy who in all these years has never been cited by the NCAA for any form of cheating. His player graduation rate is at the top among all NCAA schools and his list of credits are endless."

Billy Ray Cassidy played for Adolph Rupp on the 1958 NCAA championship team and he coached my high school basketball team. He coached just like Rupp. He screamed at us. He got in our faces at every half time of our high school games especially if we were playing bad. We saw Cassidy cuss like a sailor, scream, kick chairs, and get in our faces. And truthfully I was scared of the guy at times. But Cassidy had such a good heart. He visited me when I was in the hospital and brought me books to read. He once took me to the optometrist and bought contact lenses for me to wear because he thought I needed them.

Wayman Tisdale played on the 1984 Olympic basketball team that Knight coached. He was asked what animal Knight was most like and Tisdale said, "a pussycat."

On the flip side of this, I don't think that style of communication is necessary to get the job done in life.

We have another Hoosier who did all right in the coaching profession and he never had to pull the antics of an Adolph Rupp or Bobby Knight and that is John Wooden. He won ten championships at UCLA. What a likeable guy John Wooden is and his teams played so hard for him.

Here are some spiritual chocolates—rich delightful truths from God's word that is good for any heart! Proverbs 15:1, "A gentle answer turns away wrath, but a harsh word stirs up anger." Do you want to get something stirred up? Use harsh words. Talk ugly to somebody. Get loud or mean with someone, and the Bible says it stirs up anger.

But look what else this delight says, "A gentle answer turns away wrath." Truthfully I don't think anybody likes to be yelled at, talked down to or verbally berated. It's not the way we make friends and influence people in a positive way.

Find a good word to say!

James 3:9, "With the tongue we praise our Lord and Father, and with it we curse men, who have been made in God's likeness. Out of the same mouth come praise and cursing. My brothers, this should not be. Can both fresh water and salt water flow from the same spring? My brothers, can a fig tree bear olives, or a grapevine bear figs? Neither can a salt spring produce fresh water."

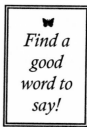

Here are a couple of thoughts: Find a good word to say! People live in stressed out environments, or work in difficult places, or things are hard at school. Find a good word to say. You are around people all the time who need a good word.

Consider the power of words. A gentle answer turns away wrath. That's powerful. Or, a harsh word stirs up anger. That's powerful. In other words you have the ability to make somebody mad or glad.

It's all by the words that we choose to use. James says in chapter 3 that a ship may be large and driven by strong winds, but they are steered by a very small rudder.

Think of how groups and assemblies have been steered by the power of words. Or think about a classroom of children and how they are affected by teachers' words, compliments or even criticisms. A good word may make a student, but a word wrongly used could be a major setback for a child.

James 3:5 says, "Consider what a great forest is set on fire by a small spark." We have heard it said before it only takes a spark to get a fire going. One wrongly used word may start a chain reaction of gossip that is totally untrue and the result of that may be a devastated life.

So our words have power. They have the power to curse or the power to bless. They have the power to build up or the power to tear down. They have the power to help or the power to hurt.

Consider the unspoken word. Sometimes it's better to say nothing, because there are occasions when we don't know what to say. So it's better to say nothing than to try to make something up. James 1:26, "If anyone considers himself religious and yet does not keep a tight rein on his tongue, he deceives himself and his religion is worthless."

Sometimes though, it's a sin when we do not speak. Here is somebody maybe really being maligned and put down. And maybe we know the truth about that person. And we should say, no, wait . . . I happen to know the truth about that situation and so here is my take on that.

People don't know for sure unless we use words. There is a guy I know who has great difficulty talking. He uses an instrument that he puts over his throat but rarely does he use it. Most of the time it's just a wave of his hand and that's it. But you know, before that guy had surgery he complained about everything. He was ugly at times. And now even if he wanted to go back and clean up some of the nasty things that he said I think it would be hard. He would have to write them out for people to read. He wouldn't be able to use words.

People don't always know for sure unless we tell them. Do you really think a lot of your children? Tell them. And tell them again.

One evening I knew I would not hang up the phone from talking to my dad without saying these words, "Dad, I love you." And he was quick to tell me "I love you, too." At that time he was facing surgery—and an aneurysm of the aorta is a wake up call. There is always the fear of not surviving the surgery. In our case there was the fear he would not make it even to the time of surgery.

Our wives need to hear everyday that we love them and husbands need to hear it too. People at work need a good word. Try it and see if it changes things any at all. Let them hear a good word from you. "You're a good worker. You're an upbeat person. You always are a motivating force here at work."

Good words are like chocolates and you can't get enough. A bad word is like an old outdated soft drink. Who needs it? Do you? Do you need bad words?

In the church we need to encourage others too. Thank you for all that you do. Our church needs you. You are a blessing to our church. Your attendance here makes our church better. You are a great help or an inspiration. I greatly appreciate you.

And we think, "Oh they know that." No they don't for sure. "Well I told them yesterday and I'll let them know if anything changes." Good words are like chocolates and you can't get enough. A bad word is like an old outdated soft drink. Who needs it? Do you? Do you need bad words?

How about a good word? Here is a good word for you. God loves you and has a wonderful plan for your life. Share His love with others.

CHAPTER THREE
REFLECTION AND MEDITATION

1. Have you spoken harsh words to anyone?

2. How do you feel when someone is verbally abusive to you?

3. According to James chapter three, what are some of the abilities of our words?

4. How may we fail by not using words?

CHAPTER FOUR

Appointments

Did you ever break an appointment? Have you ever cancelled a doctor's appointment? Lunch date? Have you ever stood somebody up for a date? Just didn't show up? I think that's the worse to tell somebody I'll meet you for lunch or dinner and you don't show up.

What are some of the more important appointments that we keep? What about a job interview? Would you keep that appointment? I once advertised for someone to be a caregiver to my wife. I had over 100 calls in response to that ad. However, I had a number of people who never showed up for the interview. But there were some who made a very special effort to make it.

What about your wedding appointment? If you are supposed to get married next weekend you likely are to make it. I've heard on rare occasions of brides and grooms being stood up at the altar—what a tragedy and embarrassment.

What about important occasions such as the birth of a child, or your child's graduation from school or a birthday party or anniversary occasion?

What if the IRS said we want to talk to you next week at a certain time? Bring your records. Are you going to keep that appointment?

There are some appointments we take seriously. There are some appointments we may ignore. There are some appointments we may break and others we may reschedule. But there is one appointment that we will not break and we would be a little crazy if we ignore, and that is the appointment with death.

Hebrews 9:27, "Just as man is destined to die once, and after that to face judgment." Please understand I've not come to this section of the book to be morbid or make you feel like you should be wringing your hands in fear about death.

We can approach death all kinds of ways. We can ignore the matter altogether, although it won't go away. It is ever coming closer and closer. The moment that we are born, we begin to die.

We can just close our minds to the subject and pretend that it's never going to happen to us. We can do this by never thinking about it—always being busy. We can just imagine that it's something that is just a thousand years away for us. It doesn't change the reality of the fact that we are going to die. But we can live thinking that way probably right up until the moment we breathe our last breath.

Secondly, you can live in fear and anxiety every day. You can spend every waking hour wringing your hands about being in an accident or developing a progressive illness that might take your very life.

Or third, you can realize that death is going to occur and you can do all that you know to do to prepare for death and then live the best you can until that moment happens. I think the third option is the best choice.

The appointment with death is never quite clear to us. Why do all of the people involved in horrible plane crashes die? And, why are there sometimes survivors? Was it just their time to go? Was it *not* some other person's time to die?

Are we on our own clocks that are just ticking away until they end at a certain time and that's it for us? Do we have no control over our longevity?

Well God has given us a number of graces to extend our lives and care for our lives. We know there are certain lifestyles we may live that might shorten our lives.

I know that if my dad had elected not to have surgery when he was diagnosed with an aneurysm . . . he might already be in heaven. But God rose up a very capable surgeon who may have extended his life for maybe many more years. Still, he has an appointment with death.

We can end our lives. King Saul of the Old Testament saw his death coming and fell on his sword as read in 1 Samuel 31. In the New Testament Judas was so filled with despair and misery he hung himself. If you try hard enough you can take your life.

Sometimes we can be on the verge of death and rally back and get another chance. We read about Lazarus in the New Testament in John 11 who had been dead four days. The Lord brought him back. Jesus brought him back to show His power over the grave.

I kind of think my wife is Lazarus's sister. In 1998 we thought she was dying but she rallied. In May of 2000 I thought she was all but dead and she rallied. Again in October of 2000 I feared she was gone but she rallied.

I told her, "Karen, forget about this dying business; God wants you here. And whenever He is finished with you He will take you home to be with Him."

My Dad and I were in the hospital talking after his surgery to remove an aneurysm and we were rejoicing that God might give him ten or fifteen years. And he reminded me about Hezekiah great King of Judah where the Lord said, "Go back and tell Hezekiah, the leader of my people, 'This is what the Lord, the God of your father David, says: I have heard your prayer and seen your tears; I will heal you. On the third day from now you will go up to the temple of the Lord. I will add fifteen years to your life. And I will deliver you and this city from the hand of the king of Assyria. I will defend this city for my sake and for the sake of David." (2 Kings 20:5-6)

We Don't Really Understand Death

We know the body stops functioning and life from the body is gone. But what happens after we breathe our last breath?

In Luke 16, Lazarus was carried by the angels and was comforted in Abraham's bosom. Will angels come and show us the way? Does God provide a heavenly escort?

In the Old Testament Elijah was caught up to heaven in a chariot of fire and he ascended into the heavens, (2 Kings 2:11). Sounds like Elijah was on a trip.

Angels accompanied Jesus as He ascended into heaven. God in selective ways utilizes His angels in the other realm. An angel appeared to Mary and announced the birth of Christ. Angels were at the tomb to greet the women who went that day to anoint the body of Jesus, as found in Luke 24.

Will angels greet you when you begin to step out of this body and into eternity? The Bible teaches it is a great possibility. Throughout the Bible they offered this salutation, "Fear not." And maybe the first words you will hear are, "Fear not." Don't be afraid, we are here to take you to be with God. That will be an awesome trip.

Or maybe we just close our eyes here and open them in the presence of Jesus. The Bible says in 2 Corinthians chapter 5, "Therefore we are always confident and know that as long as we are at home in the body we are away from the Lord." We very likely begin with a shout of exclamation when we step onto the other side.

We Don't Understand Everything That Happens

We don't understand what people are doing after death, but here are some thoughts on the matter. The

Bible tells us that people who die *in* the Lord and with a *right relationship with Jesus Christ* are in a marvelous place, and that they are being comforted, and if there are any tears or sorrow, God is taking care of that as referred to in Revelation 7:17. There is no more sorrow and there is happiness that our minds cannot comprehend.

The Bible talks about a place of rewards. Paul said there is laid up for me a crown of righteousness and Jesus talked about many houses and mansions. We can spend all day just basking in all the splendors that await us on the other side with Christ.

The Bible also tells us that those who die *outside* of Christ don't fare so well. One man in Luke 16 is described to be in horrible torment and separated from God and loved ones. Hell is described as a place of darkness, loneliness, and suffering. Friend, who needs that? We have enough hell in this world. In this world we have so many lonely people living in darkness and who suffer physically, emotionally or in other ways. Who would want an eternity of that?

We Don't Understand Completely the End of This Life

We can't imagine it fully—not being alive in this world. We've seen dead bodies in caskets and we have buried loved ones. We have some feel for it but not fully.

We have trouble with comprehending that we don't have forever. Life is a vapor and there is but a step between death and us. We think life is never going to end.

So what should we do? Be sure you are ready to die. You are not ready to live until you are ready to die. When you can say, *I know* where I will spend eternity. When you can say, I *know* that I am saved from having to spend an eternity of despair separated from God. Then you are ready to live.

Romans 10:13, "Everyone who calls on the name of the Lord will be saved."

Romans 10:9, "That if you confess with your mouth, 'Jesus is Lord,' and believe in your heart that God raised him from the dead, you will be saved."

Acts 16:31, "Believe in the Lord Jesus, and you will be saved."

Until you die God has a plan for your life. Jeremiah 29:11, "For I know the plans I have for you . . ." God gave you a life. And God someday will take it away. Until that appointment day comes make the most of your life.

Sin, bad habits, wrong attitudes, living in discord with someone are all cancers that eat away at our wonderful life that God has given to us.

Live each day fully. Do the best you can to make a difference in this life. Help others. Be a benefit to your church and your family and your community and fellowman. Make adjustments so that you may enjoy life to the fullest.

Sin, bad habits, wrong attitudes, living in discord with someone are all cancers that eat away at our wonderful life that God has given to us.

Lamentations 3:40, "Let us examine our ways and test them, and let us return to the Lord."

Psalm 90:12 "Teach *us* to number our days aright, that we may gain a heart of wisdom." We number our days so we know we don't have forever. We don't have forever to live purposeful lives. We don't have forever to love and to be useful.

Sometimes this requires an awakening. Sometimes this requires a re-evaluation of our lives. Sometimes this requires an examination of our hearts.

God has provided us with the light that life is short. He has also given to us spiritual insights and plain truth from His word to make this life, with all of its ups and downs, a rich and rewarding experience for all who will reach into the box of chocolate and take His delights that inspire and delight the human heart.

CHAPTER FOUR
REFLECTION AND MEDITATION

1. How many appointments do you have this week?

2. What are the most important appointments?

3. How do we prepare for our final appointment on earth?

CHAPTER FIVE

Success Begins With Belief Followed By Hard Work!

There is always a price to pay for success. Nothing comes easy or overnight. Often the success we enjoy has come after tedious weeks or months and even years of labor. But we must believe in what we are doing and believe with God's help that we can do it.

The school counselor may say to the student, "If you study now you'll get a better job later." So the student sacrifices ballgames and bull sessions on the telephone in order to study and have financial freedom later.

The athlete works hard in the gym dedicating hours to sweating and working the muscles because the great athlete's have learned, "No pain—no gain."

I think of some of the ladies I know who are pregnant and all they are going through to bring a child into this world. Mothers endure the hardship and the pain because they are expectant.

When we struggle and go through a valley in life, we are tempted to quit. We give up. We give up on life, friends, family and God and think they all let us down. People get bitter instead of better. They don't grow through the hardship or difficulty but regress in life sometimes turning to drugs binging on alcohol, or even suicide.

The only President who didn't use the Bible for his oath of office was Franklin Pierce. The reason was his son was killed in a train wreck on the way to the inauguration. Pierce was so angry with God that he refused to swear on the Bible.

A mother one time dropped out of church completely because her teenage daughter became pregnant out of wedlock. She was embarrassed about it, but even more was angry with God for letting that happen.

Dr. Charles Elliott was born with a horrible birthmark covering half his face. This otherwise perfect child had this terrible purple disfigurement on half his face. His mother protected him but she dreaded the day he went to school. He came home the first day sobbing, "Mommy the other kids made fun of me and stared at me." His mother said, "Charles if you will study hard they will respect you." Years later Dr. Charles Elliott was President of Harvard University. And he said, "The turning point in his life came when his mother said, "Charles there are some things in life that you cannot change, no matter how hard you try you have to accept them and you have to work through them."

Dave Drevecky, who played major league baseball, lost his pitching arm to cancer. He said he was standing on the top of Pikes Peak admiring the beauty when suddenly he realized that almost no vegetation grows beyond eleven thousand feet on the mountain. He said there is almost no growth on the mountaintop. The growth occurs in the valley. He said almost everybody wants to be on the mountaintop, but the growth occurs in the valley.

No one wants to live in the valley. We long for the mountain top experiences of life. But the valleys and difficulties of life often bring about a positive purpose.

The doctor says, "You have to have this surgery. It will be painful. But it will extend your life for a number of years." So you endure the pain so that you can experience improved health.

As we all face struggles and difficulties every day remember the following:

Success is the result of a goal and planning on how we might achieve the goal. Success seldom happens apart from hard work.

Don't give up! The darkest part of night always comes before daybreak. When life seems dark and hopeless you are probably close to the light you've been hoping for.

Finally, you must believe! You might conceive the idea of accomplishing a great project but without genuine belief in your heart that it can be done, it will never become a reality. Jesus said, "Everything is possible for him who believes." (Mark 9:23)

CHAPTER FIVE
REFLECTION AND MEDITATION

1. How productive are you when living on the mountaintop?

2. How is your valley shaping your life?

3. Will you let God make something useful of your valley experience? How?

CHAPTER SIX

God Is Amazing!

What does it take to impress you? We live in an age today where we have seen, heard, and experienced so much that our senses sometimes get a little dulled.

I grew up in a home where the only clear television station we could get on a black and white television was WSAZ in Huntington, West Virginia. As a child I remember knowing what was on television. Usually if I wanted to watch TV, I watched whatever was on; and sometimes the programs were a little boring. Then I remember when we were able to pick up the ABC affiliate and I couldn't believe the variety I had. Sometimes it was hard to decide if I wanted to watch *The Man from Uncle* . . . or the *Monkees*.

Cable came along and today the television channels seem almost unlimited. You know what I do sometimes? I'll take that remote and go through almost every channel just to see what's on. Most of the time I think, "Oh well, nothing's on television tonight." And yet there are fifty channels and all of them offer some form of news programs or entertainment. You may not have cable and you pick up three or four local stations in your area. You are content with that because maybe you just don't care that much about watching television. There are days when I can certainly understand that.

When I was a young teenager, McDonald's restaurants were few and far between in East, Kentucky. I think the first McDonald's I ate in was in Ashland. I was a teenager and I was amazed at how good a Big Mac was and what I could buy for a dollar. But you know, I haven't eaten a Big Mac since May of 1994 . . . and I am not that interested in eating a Big Mac. I'm sure they are just as good today as they were then but we have more competition now. We have Whoppers, and Big Bacon Classics and Sonic Burgers and Rally Burgers and truthfully most of the time I don't feel impressed to eat any of them.

Moderation in some things use to be a problem for me especially when I had a better metabolism that kept churning. When I was a kid, one time I ate five J Boys. Have you ever eaten a J Boy? Jerry's restaurants are still around in a few places and they offer a J Boy sandwich and they aren't bad.

But truthfully, I haven't eaten a J Boy sandwich in most likely ten years. Somebody says, "Let's go have a J Boy." Naw . . . that doesn't turn me on.

How has your life changed? What is there about life that no longer impresses you or excites you? You may have once had a real zeal for your vocation and thought wow this is the job of my dreams. Then after a few years you may have started thinking, "I'm not so crazy about this work anymore . . . surely there is something else I can do with my life." Sometimes we lose our enthusiasm.

Maybe you felt having four or five kids would be the fulfillment of your life. And then after about fifteen years and about seven or eight thousand loads of laundry you say, "Well it's been great and I wouldn't have traded them for the world, but it's time now to move on with life."

My mother didn't have an automatic washing machine until I was about 13 or 14 years old. There were five kids at home. She did the laundry and dried the clothes on a clothesline and ironed everything. It was a Monday, Tuesday and Wednesday job every week. Three full days that's about all she could do. I think after five kids my mother probably no longer felt any strong impressions to have any more.

God never changes. And God has to do nothing to keep our attention nor does He have to do any new tricks to impress us.

Life has cycles and transitions. We have highs and lows. We are one way in life for a season and then we change and have different feelings or impressions. But, God never changes. And God has to do nothing to keep our attention nor does He have to do any new tricks to impress us. Yet there is nothing about this Holy God that is unimpressive . . . He is truly an amazing God!

The New Testament story in Matthew chapter one is filled with amazement. First we are reminded here that people dream. Verse 19 of the chapter says, "Mary was pledged to be married to Joseph . . ." Mary and Joseph were engaged. They were planning on the wedding and being husband and wife and pursuing all the dreams that any young couple might have starting out . . . love, romance, career and children.

I think everybody at one time or another has some kind of dream. It may be in the engagement that you have to someone. It may be in your work. Your dream may be in your pursuit of your education or your new freedom in your retirement.

We never grow too old, too sick or too down trodden to dream. Sometimes the cares and adversities of life steal from us our dream. And what happens is we begin to perish. Proverbs says, "Where there is no vision the people perish." Vision is looking forward. You can't go forward looking back. You can't drive your car looking over your shoulder because you are bound for disaster. You must dream and work toward that which is better. I want to challenge you to keep dreaming for your life. God has plenty in store for you if you will let God rule in your life. God is Amazing!

God is an amazing God because He brings about a quality of life that our dreams could never fathom. The Baby Jesus was a real live baby who had nothing but an incredible life in front of Him. And, in His death He would save a world of people from lives of despair and give each of us forgiveness of our sins and eternal life. God is Amazing!

Secondly, life changes. Mary and Joseph are going to be married as husband and wife. They have had a very proper wholesome engagement. They have saved sex for the marriage union. And then Mary says, "Joseph I'm pregnant."

> *God is an amazing God because He brings about a quality of life that our dreams could never fathom.*

"You're what?"

"Yes, I'm pregnant. But it's okay, Joseph. It's all of the Holy Spirit."

"Mary what kind of pills have you been taking? This is crazy, Mary. I can't believe you have done this to our relationship. It's off. It's all off."

Joseph was going to be kind about it. The Bible says because Joseph was a righteous man and did not want to expose her to public disgrace, he had in mind to divorce her quietly," Matthew 1:19.

There are times when life changes. We talked about dreams. Mary and Joseph didn't dream this one. They had not planned to begin their marriage relationship this way. But guess what? Plans change. Life changes. Who in a thousand years would have dreamed something like this up? God. God would and He did. Friend, God is Amazing!

Galatians 4:4, "But when the time had fully come, God sent his Son, born of a woman, born under law, to redeem those under law, that we might receive the full rights of sons." The change of life for Mary and Joseph at the time had to be overwhelming. How might all this be perceived? What would people say? And what one young couple started out thinking would be a normal married blissful existence turned out to be quite a life. Being parents to God. God chose two peasant young people to fulfill His promise of coming to this world. God is Amazing!

So Mary and Joseph had a life changing event and that was raising God's Son—who was God in the flesh.

God is amazing. He totally changed Mary and Joseph's life. They never dreamed life would be like it would become for them. And, chances are your life will go through unexpected joys, celebrations and even adversities like you cannot imagine. Life changes. God is Amazing!

God Intervenes

Verse twenty of Mathew chapter one says, "But after he had considered this, an angel of the Lord appeared to him in a dream and said, "Joseph, son of David, do not be afraid to take Mary home as your wife, because what is conceived in her is from the Holy Spirit. She will give birth to a son, and you are to give him the name Jesus, because he will save his people from their sins."

Don't you wish it were always this easy? Joseph has come to a crossroads in his life. He has a conscience . . . he wants to do what is right, but he is not going to live with some immoral spouse that has been unfaithful to him. God intervenes and in a dream affirms to Joseph what Mary told him to be the truth.

Wouldn't it be wonderful if God would just tell us all in our dreams tonight exactly what we need to do? If He would only tell us about a certain decision or life changing event or where He would have us to go to school or who to date or marry or our service to Him, or a decision we have to make about retirement. Or if God would just intervene and write something in the sky for us to read or allow some event to take place in our lives that would confirm a feeling that we have or that would show us the way.

God intervened in the lives of Mary and Joseph in dramatic fashion. God is Amazing! But why doesn't He do that today? I think God does more than we know.

In May of 1989 Karen and I were so hurt and angry with God when we buried our stillborn son Jesse Caleb in Paintsville, Kentucky. But, Karen could never have really cared for that baby because she starting fighting multiple sclerosis less than a year later when Zachary was only five and Jared was eight. I think it may have been God's way of saying, "Karen, you have your hands full . . . I'm going to bring this one home to be with me." Bill Messer stood at the grave with us that day and said,

"This child will reach his full potential in heaven." And he will. He will be there for us to enjoy for all eternity.

Has God ever intervened in your life? Of course He has. One day God led me to Bible school and there I came to know Jesus as my Lord and personal savior. That one little trip to Bible school changed my life and gave me a whole new purpose for living. I've met more people—great people, in the house of God all over this world than I would have ever known had it not been for God's intervention. God is Amazing!

God may have saved you in Korea, or Vietnam, or WWII. For some of you, God intervened and saved your marriage or saved you from a life of addiction or destructive behavior. I think God is more at work than what we realize or give Him credit for. He intervened in the life of Joseph and He is at work in our lives today. God is Amazing!

Mary and Joseph were obedient to God. In Matthew 1:24, "When Joseph woke up, he did what the angel of the Lord had commanded him and took Mary home as his wife. But he had no union with her until she gave birth to a son. And he gave him the name, Jesus."

Joseph could have pulled a Jonah and said, "Nope I'm out of here. I'm going to be free of all of this." God found two people that He could use and who would obey Him.

Jesus said, "If anyone loves me, he will obey my teaching," (John 14:23). God is looking for people today who love Him and will obey Him. It only makes sense that God can use those and bless those who obey Him.

Let's say you have a child that lives in constant rebellion toward you. You love that child and you want to help that child but you can't as long as that child has that kind of attitude.

God wants to help us and bless us. But if we live in constant unrepentant rebellion toward Him, there is no way under the sun that He is going to, excuse this expression, break His neck to help us. And, we can't blame Him.

Proverbs 6:16, "There are six things the Lord hates, seven that are detestable to him: haughty eyes, a lying tongue, hands that shed innocent blood, a heart that devices wicked schemes, feet that are quick to rush into evil, a false witness who pours out lies and a man who stirs up dissension among brothers." "The Bible says these are detestable to God. If you are making God sick with such a disobedient wayward lifestyle why would you expect God to richly bless you?

Mary and Joseph were two vessels that God could use and were obedient to Him. God Produced a Miracle. Mary gave birth to Jesus. To more fully understand the impact of this miracle you have to look at John chapter 1 where the Bible says in verse one, "In the beginning was the Word, and the Word was with God, and the Word was God. And then in verse 14, "The Word became flesh and made his dwelling among us."

God did a miracle and God still does miracles today. He is doing miracles in people's hearts and families and churches. We need all three today. God can still work a miracle in your life and in your family. But our hearts have to be right. We have to be open, we have to be believing and obedient and we have to be available. God has never stopped working miracles. The angel Gabriel said to Mary, "For nothing is impossible with God." God is Amazing!

God still uses people today to accomplish His work and perform His miracles. God used Mary and Joseph and God will use you.

Who are the spiritual giants at your church? Who are the Joshuas and Calebs who are saying come on let's take the city, let's take the mountain . . . let's go forward! Who are the Davids in your church who will say, give me Goliath, I don't care how big he is; God is bigger! Who are those who are like Moses in your church that will say, yes that's a big river, but God will help us to walk across it; God is bigger! Who are those like Zacchaeus in your church who have had such life changing experiences after meeting Jesus, that business and vocation and all of life has been dramatically changed? Who are the women that have met Jesus at the well and had a talk with Jesus and now are able to say, see this man who told me all things . . . who knows all things? Or who are the men and women whose lives were ravaged by sin like the woman who was about to be stoned? Jesus stepped in and saved her and then He said,

"Go now and leave your life of sin." (John 8:12) All of these men and women were people that God used because *God is Amazing!* And God is still using people today.

God Keeps His Promises

Jesus Christ came into the world. The centuries rolled by. Prophets had foretold so many years before and I am sure people could have easily given up. But no matter how long the time of waiting may be, it should encourage every Christian to believe more firmly that God keeps His promises no matter how long the time of waiting may be.

You see friend, God has not left the world to run automatically. God is involved in His world. All the births in all the centuries would never have produced the Son of God. Only by the divine act of intervention into the human process, by the miraculous conception of Jesus through the Holy Spirit, did the Son of God become a man . . . to live, be tempted, suffer, and die for you.

God keeps His promise in regard to all of life. He promised He would be with us always. And, He is. He promised us eternal life and nothing can take that away. He promised us the Holy Spirit who lives inside each believer today. And He helps us day by day.

Friend, isn't God amazing? Delight yourself this very day in this Amazing Powerful God!

CHAPTER SIX
REFLECTION AND MEDITATION

1. God never changes. How has God remained the constant unchanging God in your life?

2. How has life changed for you in the last twelve months?

3. How would you like for life to change in the next twelve months?

4. How will you look to God to meet the needs of your changing life?

CHAPTER SEVEN

Help Others

Then He turned to His disciples and said privately, "Blessed are the eyes that see what you see. For I tell you that many prophets and kings wanted to see what you see but did not see it, and to hear what you hear but did not hear it."

On one occasion an expert in the law stood up to test Jesus. "Teacher," he asked, "what must I do to inherit eternal life?"

"What is written in the Law?" he replied. "How do you read it?"

He answered: "'Love the Lord your God with all your heart and with all your soul and with all your strength and with all your mind;' and, 'Love your neighbor as yourself.'" (Luke 10:23–37)

Let's study three kinds of people in this Bible passage. There are people who will hurt you. There are people who are physically dangerous. This man was beaten, robbed and left for dead. We lock our doors to our homes. We are careful about walking in neighborhoods that have a reputation for violence. If you are driving in some cities you lock the doors to your car out of fear. It's almost daily that we read the newspaper about someone being killed, maimed, or physically accosted in some way.

People can be dangerous in other ways. People can hurt you with words. We've heard the old saying, sticks and stones may break my bones but words will never hurt me. But the truth is that words *do* hurt.

It may be that you can say something about someone that is incorrect and it can be repeated a dozen times and usually expanded with each new version. But seldom can the damage be repaired.

There are people in life that will ignore you. I think we may have a lot of that in our society. We've gotten good at the ignoring game.

Years ago when the phones would ring in the evening we would answer them expecting somebody to be on the other end. Recently a computer called and said somebody wanted to talk to me but they were busy and wanted to know if I would wait just a minute until they had the time to talk to me. Crazy?

So when we hear from all these telephone solicitors we become pretty good at saying "no thanks . . . not today." Because if we don't we will spend our evenings on the phone talking to one right after another.

We've become calloused in other areas. We see so much human need. And there are so many charities. There are so many organizations to help. We know that most of them are good, but we know we can't help them all and therefore many people don't help any.

The Salvation Army comes out in full force during the Christmas season. You can't put money in every pot. Our society has become so accustomed to them that I wonder how many people never really take notice and ignore them altogether.

I wonder how many members of my church totally ignore giving anything to our church? People, who come week after week, have paying jobs and give nothing.

What are those aspects of life that we just turn off? We turn off the television when we want quiet. We change the phone number when we tire of harassing calls. We quietly pull away if there is a matter in life we don't want to deal with and try to ignore it.

There are the people in life who help others. In my home church we have a lot of helpers . . . people that help out in so many ways. They help other members with tasks and situations in life.

We have a lot of manual workers in my church—people who will manually put their hands to the plow and help a neighbor out in time of need.

We have some listeners in the church—people who will be there to listen to you . . . if you just need a listener.

We have awesome prayer warriors in my church—people who will pray with you about your burdens and cares.

We have many encouragers in the church—folks who have a good word to brighten your day.

We have many who sacrifice a lot. There are people who sacrifice in giving financially and serving in different capacities in the life of the church.

I can think of a lot of helpers over my lifetime. I thought of Virgil Moore the other day. Virgil was my fifth grade school teacher and weighed about 400 pounds. He was my basketball coach until I was in the sixth grade. Mr. Moore always had us involved in projects. He would have us giving speeches. We could give a speech about most anything. Sometimes he would have us sing in class and he didn't care what we sang. Or he got involved in our 4-H projects and would have us demonstrate them in class. He was a teacher who was always trying to help a student unleash their talent and see their potential.

I think Good Samaritans are those who take the time to stop along the way and do whatever they can to help. This good man did more than the religious people did who passed by and ignored this beaten man. He was compassionate and did everything that he could do. He helped the man physically and financially. He went the extra mile. He did more than just the average person.

> *Good Samaritans are those who take the time to stop along the way and do whatever they can to help.*

I think that's the most that God expects out of us and that's the most that we can expect out of people. To have compassion—which comes from the heart, to do what we can do when helping others.

CHAPTER SEVEN
REFLECTION AND MEDITATION

1. Who is someone that has helped you in life?

2. Who is someone that you might be a Good Samaritan to?

3. Help comes in various forms. Name some of the different methods of helping others.

CHAPTER EIGHT

How to Move From Here to There!

When they came to the crowd, a man approached Jesus and knelt before him. Lord, have mercy on my son," he said. "He has seizures and is suffering greatly. He often falls into the fire or into the water. I brought him to your disciples, but they could not heal him."

O unbelieving and perverse generation," Jesus replied, "how long shall I stay with you? How long shall I put up with you? Bring the boy here to me." Jesus rebuked the demon, and it came out of the boy, and he was healed from that moment.

Then the disciples came to Jesus in private and asked, "Why couldn't we drive it out?"

He replied, "Because you have so little faith. I tell you the truth, if you have faith as small as a mustard seed, you can say to this mountain, 'Move from here to there' and it will move. Nothing will be impossible for you." (Matthew 17:14–21)

Jesus came preaching and teaching possibility. He told the disciples, "Nothing will be impossible for you." The angel assured Mary in Luke's gospel, "For nothing is impossible with God." And I believe all of us would say "Amen," God can do anything. Nothing is impossible with the one who spoke and the heavens came into reality. But I think most of us, most of the time, are like the weak disciples. Look what it says; they came to Jesus in private. That's what we would do . . . and they asked, "Why couldn't we drive it out?" The father had approached the disciples and he left sighing and defeated . . . they could not heal him.

Do you ever feel like that? "I went to my friend and he couldn't help me." Or, "I went to my Sunday school class and they couldn't help." I went to the pastor and he tried, but he couldn't help either."

Notice this man in this scripture went directly to Jesus. And no one can do any more for you than Jesus. We all need people to talk to; but you have no other such a friend or brother than Jesus. Try taking it directly to Jesus.

You may know how this father felt. You may know how the disciples felt. The father is a broken hearted daddy. My child . . . my son needs help. Who will help my son? Disciples, men of God, will you help my son?

Have you ever been there? Sometimes we say, "Help! My son needs extra attention, counseling, help or support." Or, "my daughter is pregnant and needs help!" Or, "I have a child struggling in school or in relationships." In some way we have all been there or we are there now.

Jesus of course is the hero in this story because He in quick fashion takes care of the problem. The Bible says the boy was healed from that moment. This is quite a story. It was a quick answer for a struggling dad and a hurting son. But I think there is more to this story than fast miracles and quick fixes because Jesus talked about a tiny seed and He talked about moving mountains. He said if you have faith as small as a mustard seed, you can say to this mountain, move from here to there and it will move.

Do you have any mountains that need moving? Sometimes moving a mountain means changing the direction of your life and turning it around. Sometimes moving a mountain is resolving a conflict or a problem. Sometimes moving a mountain is working things out in our daily work or career lives. Sometimes a mountain is a marriage relationship or making a decision about another relationship.

Ideas are dreams trying to break into reality!

But Jesus talked about moving mountains from here to there. How do you get from here to there? How do you move the mountain from here to there?

It begins with an idea. Ideas are dreams trying to break into reality! Not all dreams come true. Not all dreams come into reality. A lot of lives are lived with a lot of ideas and dreams that never come into existence. They were just an idea. Today's realities began with an idea. Let me give you an example.

Jared and Zachary are my two sons. They are a reality. Several years ago they were an idea. Their mother and I said, "Let's have children." Our idea became realities.

Children didn't come easy for Karen and I. We had several miscarriages and there were surgeries to enhance fertilization and there was a while when we didn't think we would ever have children.

Realities begin with an idea that is a dream that sometimes becomes a mountain we are trying to move from here to there.

Our dream for a while seemed like a mountain we were trying to move. Some ideas are like dreams that are like mountains; and moving them from here to there . . . sometimes seems so impossible! We often find ourselves like the disciples—exhausted, "Lord we couldn't drive it out. Why couldn't we do it?"

Realities begin with an idea that is a dream that sometimes becomes a mountain we are trying to move from here to there. Let me give you another example.

Our church building began with a drawing. Then we had a banner made to hang in front of our congregation. The banner was just a banner. The drawing was nothing more than a drawing. The drawing was an idea. But a beautiful building over the period of about three years soon took the place of the drawings and banner. The idea became a reality.

The building began with a seed of an idea. It was an idea, a dream . . . trying to break into reality. The building did not come easy. And whenever you move a mountain from here to there, it is never easy.

Our church went from meeting in a house, to a small building, to a large multipurpose building, to a very nice expanded worship facility. It took place with much faith, with many seeds, with a lot of dreaming. Today we have the reality. Jesus said, you can move from here to there but you have to have faith, be it small as a mustard seed. You must plant it and then you can move the mountain.

Efforts are keys seeking to unlock a door of opportunity. I read about some people a few months ago that were in a contest. Each of them had a key and the opportunity to try to fit their key into a new truck. The winner of the truck would have the key that turned the ignition. In this scenario there was only one winner. But about ten of them had keys and they all showed up to see who won. You would to, I think. Here is a key and it might start a $35,000 truck . . . you would say, "Yes, let me see if it will crank it up."

Some of us from our church knock on doors of people who visit our church. Rarely do I go into someone's home that visited. I just knock on the door and say "Glad you came to church . . . hope you'll come back,"

When we do that, it's just a small effort trying to unlock and open a door of opportunity.

I was struck with the awesome decision of putting my wife into a skilled nursing facility. Financially there was no way I could afford it. Plus the emotional magnitude of the decision was overwhelming. I thought at first, with the combination of eight or ten incredible women who had been helping me from church, maybe I could hire someone part time to help out. So I ran an ad in our local paper, "Caregiver needed for invalid lady, $8 an hour." I thought, "Hope I get a call or three or four calls would be nice." The first two days I received over 60 phone calls and the calls came for over a week. I ended up getting over 100 inquiries from that one advertisement. But, I had to make that two-day $28 investment in that advertisement. And that ad obviously found a lot of lookers.

That advertisement was a mustard seed ad and that mustard seed presented a mountain of opportunity and it moved us from A to B and from here to there.

Where do you need to make an effort? Is it at home? Is it with school? Is it with your life? Is it with a soured friendship? Is it in your distant fuzzy relationship with God? Your effort may be the key that unlocks the door of opportunity.

Do what the disciples did. Those followers of Christ brought their problem to Jesus and asked, "Why couldn't we do it? Lord . . . we need your help." Persistence is the road where hope lives.

The scripture tells us this man approached Jesus and knelt before him. "Lord have mercy on my son." He brought his son. This apparently required effort. I couldn't keep from thinking about all the months of night after night of caring for my invalid wife. There was fixing a nightly shot that I injected, changing the catheter bag, changing her clothes, brushing her teeth, putting on leg braces, giving her medicine and helping her to get positioned in bed. And then in the morning doing it all over again. This man brought his son and it may likely have required effort.

> *Persistence is the road where hope lives.*

A lot of effort and persistence is going on in this verse of scripture. He goes to Jesus. He could have said, "No, he's not approachable." Or, "He's busy and I'm busy." He knelt before Jesus. He humbled himself and this was after already trying the disciples. He kept at it. He was persistent. He didn't give up hope.

When you are in school, it's hard and sometimes boring. A lot of the time you don't want to be there. But be persistent knowing someday you will no longer be in school and all that you have done will pay off in life, work and career. Keep going and doing your best. And you will move the mountain from here to there. Because persistence is the road where hope lives.

Treatment and medicine are strange. When you love somebody, you hang in there and keep trying. I saw a friend of mine at the nursing home with his wife. I know he went every day . . . helping her eat, pushing her in the wheelchair, talking to her and I knew Charlie was just exhausted. Charlie was such a good, faithful and persistent husband.

My wife and I have bought so much medicine. Where there is sickness you just keep trying. When we got the drug Betaseron in May of 1994, we tore that package open and thought this is it. This is going to fix Karen's health. We didn't care that it was a $1000 a month. We used it for over 2 years. Then we tried Avonex another drug for MS and that went on for over two years. And now we do Copaxone every day, about an $800 a month drug.

Why? Persistence is the road where hope lives. Persistence doesn't give up. You want to. It's mind over matter and faith over emotions and it's mountains that sometimes are just so big.

I suppose the biggest mountain I've ever seen was in Kenya, Africa. But the mountains out around Salt Lake City are very huge, too. I've often wondered how early settlers ever had the nerve to even try going over them. But they did with difficulty and much persistence because they had hope of something better on the other side as a result of their hard work and persistence.

Is there something about your life where your hope has dwindled? Persistence is the road where hope lives. You see you haven't given up. You keep trying to get on top of your game. You keep trying to make the passing grade. You don't give up. And yes even though we feel like this man in this scripture sometimes, we come to Christ saying, "Lord have mercy on me and help me!" Jesus says, "Keep planting your faith." Although it may be small, keep planting your faith. Keep believing and hoping.

Patience is our friend who walks the journey with us. These disciples had each other and most importantly they had Jesus. But look at this father in this scripture. He's got to be losing it. "My boy has seizures. He falls into the fire or into the water. He is suffering greatly. My son is really having a hard time."

When I was in high school we had a student who it seemed about once a month would have a full-blown seizure. Several times it happened in the gymnasium with several hundred students watching Ricky's body go through the most horrible contortions.

We had a teacher in school whose name was Mr. Haney. He only had one arm because he lost it working at a sawmill. But Mr. Haney would stretch Ricky out on one of the bleachers of the gym and sit there with him until that seizure wore off. I remember how quiet it would get in that gym. Later I would see Ricky get up and walk off to class and he would always be alone. People were nice to him. But I never saw anybody hanging around him. It spoke volumes about Mr. Haney who sometimes it seemed appeared from nowhere and who would stay by his side until he was alright.

This daddy in this scripture was at wits end but patiently he is hanging in there with his child. "Lord, he is suffering greatly. He falls in the fire and in the water, Lord he's driving us all crazy could you help him?" Here is a persistent father who has tried to be a patient daddy and walk the journey with his child.

The Bible says, "The fruit of the Holy Spirit of God is Patience." Patience enables us to make the journey . . . with a child or a sick wife.

Isn't that like Jesus? You have no other such a friend or brother. Jesus is the friend who never leaves us or forsakes us. He is so patient with us. When we mess up He cleans us up. When we fall down He helps us up. He walks the journey of life with us helping us to do what He did for these disciples moving from here to there. Life is like that isn't it? It is a journey. And Jesus is the patient friend helping us move from here to there.

Victory is the Foundation on which we stand. As we move from here to there in whatever we do, remember our one foundation is Jesus Christ. It's from the Bible that we read, "If God be for us who can be against us? Who shall separate us from the love of Christ? Shall trouble or hardship or persecution or famine or nakedness or danger or sword? No, in all these things we are more than conquerors through him who loved us. For I am convinced that neither death nor life, neither angels nor demons, neither the present, not the future, nor any powers, neither height nor depth, nor anything else in all creation, will be able to separate us from the Love of God that is in Christ Jesus our Lord." (Romans 8:31-39)

Now, that is a foundation. Our foundation is not a flimsy, fly by night whimsical, hope it all works out religion. "Our hope is built on nothing less than Jesus' blood and righteousness; I dare not trust the sweetest frame, but wholly lean on Jesus' name. On Christ, the solid Rock I stand; all other ground is sinking sand."[2]

We take our little seed of faith and we stand on what He has done and we move our mountains from here to there.

"Encamped along the hills of light, Ye Christian soldiers, rise, and press the battle ere the night, shall veil the glowing skies. Against the foe in vales below, let all our strength be hurled; Faith is the victory, we know, that overcomes the world."[3]

Jesus won the victory by His death on the cross and His resurrection from the grave. We take our little seed of faith and we stand on what He has done and we move our mountains from here to there.

What about your life? Is it time you moved from point A to point B or to point C. This man came to Jesus and Jesus helped him. He will help you too, in whatever it is. Allow Him to work in your life beginning right now.

Who are those that you give thanks for helping you along life's way? Is it a teacher, a pastor, a friend, a parent, a church member, a classmate a neighbor, others?

---

[2] *The Solid Rock*, The Baptist Hymnal 406.
[3] *Faith is the Victory*, The Baptist Hymnal 413.

Who are those that you bless with your life by helping them? You encourage them and show them God's love. You pray for them. You help them in tangible ways. You may be a mentor to them. You inspire them. As people inspire you and are a delight to your heart you in turn enrich others. Life is not a one-way walk of gathering all that others can give to us. We in turn help others.

CHAPTER EIGHT
REFLECTION AND MEDITATION

1. Jesus proclaimed possibility. The Bible teaches with God all things are possible. What has been impossible lately for you?

2. Ideas are dreams trying to break into
_______________ .

3. A mountain of opportunity begins with us sowing a mustard seed. What seed will you plant this week?

4. Persistence is the road where hope lives. Where in your life do you need to be more persistent?

CHAPTER NINE

Life With A Plus

A man called me once saying he needed $20 to fix his car. If he had $20 he would have transportation to work and basically he was saying his life would be okay if he had $20. Financially he was broke.

I'm sure we've all had those days when $20 would have made a difference. I remember my freshman year at Southern Seminary in Louisville that if I had $20 I could survive all week . . . White Castle hamburgers wasn't far away. But I had those days going to school full time where I was like that guy who called me this week—down to lean times and trying to figure out how much I could eat for a buck. Has that ever happened to you?

I've had the opportunity to visit in a lot of homes over the last ten or twelve years where people had zero in their refrigerator. No food, bare. No Plus.

One Christmas a group of us went over to Flat Lick, Kentucky and visited in the home of a family. There were six or seven children and a baby, a husband and a wife. And all these kids slept in the same room on what appeared to be bare mattresses. We didn't see a rest room in the house and the house was pretty dirty. They were living symbols of poverty.

Poverty is living life without the common things that the average citizens of the nation enjoy. The average people in America live in comfortable houses and drive comfortable cars and have enough and usually too much food to eat and are able to enjoy some of the luxuries of life.

Poverty normally can be found in very inadequate housing. It's cold in the winter and hot in the summer. There is not a comfortable car and food is scarce. If you haven't been around abstract poverty it's hard to describe. When I tell people I know that thousands of people in our country live below the poverty level, some of them don't believe it. These people who live in such economic hardship live below the normal lot of society. How about you? Have you ever been there?

What about your car? Have you ever been driving along having a wonderful time and suddenly you look down and discover you're not only on empty, you are below empty. Or maybe your car has a voice that says, "You're almost out of gas." And we all know what a sick feeling that is to be out on an interstate and no gas stations in sight and to have our car registering below empty—in the negative.

I was with some friends for a couple of days one summer in South Dakota and we were in this rental car and just enjoying the badlands of South Dakota. We were driving along in the middle of nowhere in that barren desert of huge rock formations. And of course they don't build convenient gas stations out in the middle of nowhere. Suddenly we discovered we were on empty. Truthfully we were below empty and there was nothing in sight. It made us nervous. Here we are in the middle of nowhere and not a gasoline station in sight and we looked at the driver and said, "How could you have let this happen?" It's always good to have somebody to blame. Right? We survived it and we did manage to make it to a little country store in the middle of nowhere that sold gasoline.

Have you ever had your doctor tell you, "You are vitamin deficient"? Or, you need more Iron or more vitamin B or E or Calcium. Or, you aren't eating properly and you are anemic.

Have you ever been notified by the bank? Check number 1020 was presented but there were insufficient funds to pay it. Now you really have insufficient funds because we have just charged your account another hefty fee to really make your account in the negative. It's bad enough that your account wasn't right to cover the check and now you are even worse.

Have you ever called customer service at the bank and asked them for a balance and they said, "Your balance is a $137.50 in the negative. And you think, "How could that have happened?"

It's unsettling when the checkbook is in the negative. It starts creating an unsettling feeling when you get into below zero. The negative zone of life is a lousy feeling whether it's your gasoline tank, your personal checkbook or your ability to cope emotionally or even physically with your daily pressures.

Dr. Scott in Dayton, Ohio back in about 1975 was a VA Dentist. So his salary was fixed and he did not have an elaborate practice. But even then he gave a $100 a week to his church. He said, "I could never figure out how I would ever financially make it if I didn't give back to God." He said, "I have more than enough in every realm of my life. I've never been hungry. I've always had a nice car to drive and I've never missed the money that I gave to God."

What he said was Biblical. He said I've always had more than enough in every realm of my life. He had an amazing family. They all loved Jesus. They laughed and loved each other and went to church together. He worked hard but he was blessed.

I know that's how most of us want to live our lives. We don't like to drive the car up and down the road on a negative balance, below zero. We don't like to have a checkbook that is at zero or at a negative balance. And we don't want to live like the family I told you about earlier in abstract poverty—our children sleeping on bare mattresses, little food and struggling day by day living life in the negative.

2 Kings 4:1–7 has the story of one widow whose life had fallen into the negative. She was at zero balance in her life. Her husband was dead. He had left huge debts. The creditors were coming for the children. And she was

flat broke. In verse 2 Elisha asked, "How can I help you? Tell me, what do you have in your house?"

That's a good question. *How can I help you?* Don't ever ask that question unless you are sincere and ready to respond. Don't ask that question unless you are prepared to try to help. That's a dangerous question. Be prepared for action if you ask that question.

She responds, "Your servant has nothing there at all," I'm at zero. I'm in the negative. And then like she has this after thought, "Except a little oil." That's it.

Elisha said, "Take that little bit of oil, gather up jars—go into your house, shut the door and start pouring." And she obeyed him. The oil continued to flow until she and her son ran out of vessels. Elisha told her to sell this oil. Pay off your creditors and live on the rest. Her life was turned around from almost nothing to more than enough.

In Luke chapter 9, Jesus told His disciples to feed a massive amount of people and they said, "We don't have enough. We only have five loaves of bread and two fish." And He instructed His disciples on what to do and they obeyed Him. The Bible says all five thousand of them ate and were satisfied and over twelve baskets of food were left over. They ended up with more than enough.

God doesn't want us to live life in the negative. God wants us to live life in the plus with more than enough oil and more than enough food.

David said, "I have never seen the righteous forsaken or their children begging bread." (Psalm 37:25)

Jesus said in Matthew, "And why do you worry about clothes? See how the lilies of the field grow. They do not labor or spin. Yet I tell you that not even Solomon in all his splendor was dressed like one of these. If that is how God clothes the grass of the field, which is here today, and tomorrow is thrown into the fire, will he not much more clothe you, O you of little faith? So do not worry saying, 'What shall we eat?' or 'What shall we drink?' or 'What shall we wear?' For the pagans run after all these things and your heavenly Father knows that you need them. But seek first his kingdom and his righteousness, and all these things will be given to you as well. Therefore do not worry about tomorrow, for tomorrow will worry about itself. Each day has enough trouble of it's own." (Mathew 6:28-34)

What about you? Are you living in the negative? Not enough—minus zero balance?

Folks when you are out of gas you're in trouble. The car stops. If the airplane runs out of fuel it crashes. Have you ever heard of a plane crash because they didn't have enough fuel? It's happened.

Maybe you are on the verge of just crashing. You don't know how much longer you're going to keep the engine running. Or maybe your engine has already stopped. You're not going anywhere. Or maybe you can't go anywhere. You're like the widow . . . zero balance.

Sometimes we get this way physically. Jesus got tired. There were times He had to get away from the crowds and take a break. Elijah was exhausted after his battle with the false prophets of Baal. He was so depleted he got depressed and didn't think he could go on with life. "I'm beat Lord. Take my life."

Do you ever just get worn down and on empty? Sometimes we get this way emotionally. We get emotionally worn down with all that is happening in life. There are so many cares, problems, and troubles that we feel like the Indiana University policy code they invoked for Bobby Knight, "zero tolerance." The administration was saying, "We can't take this anymore. One more strike and you're out. After 29 years we're out of gas."

That's not a good way to live either. You may be emotionally drained from dealing with a person, a job, a situation, or some problem.

I think when Elijah went into that cave and hid and prayed to die, he was also emotionally spent from hassling with King Ahab and Jezebel. They were in constant tension and battle and stress. Emotionally that will do a number on you and the number is always zero. You don't come out with any plusses when you are in emotional gridlock. Have you got anything with anybody going on in your life that is draining the life out of you?

You can get this way financially. Things can happen that take you under. Unexpected bills, job loss, medical stress and education the list is endless.

You can get this way spiritually. I wonder how many people sit in church and look good, but they are running on the fumes—or nothing at all. Maybe you are trying to go through the motions of church on zero. There isn't much of any fuel left in your Christian tank; and if you aren't careful, you're going to just quit reading the Bible, quit praying, quit giving, quit talking to anybody about your faith in Christ, quit church and just drop out.

> *Disobedience to God results in a negative balance in our lives. Obedience results in a plus.*

Sadly, that's what has happened to probably at least half of the members in the average church. They never give anything to the church. They don't show up for anything. I doubt if they are witnessing or talking to a lot of people about their faith in Christ.

What can we do? Be Obedient—Jesus taught in John chapter fifteen the vital importance of obeying His commands.

The widow obeyed Elisha. The scriptures have a simple truth. Disobedience to God results in a negative balance in our lives. Obedience results in a plus.

Be alert. Be smart. When your life is on empty. Try to get some gas. If you are tired, find a way to rest. If you're in emotional straits with someone work for reconciliation. If you are spiritually about to end up on the rocks of despair, remember Paul said in Ephesians chapter six, "Be alert our enemy the devil is a roaring lion seeking whom he may devour. Therefore put on the whole armor of God that you may be able to stand against the devil." Be alert. Be decisive. Make decisions regarding your life, your finances, your jobs, your relationships and your walk with God.

Make a daily decision to live life in the plus. Daily determine, "As for me and my house we will serve the Lord." (Joshua 24:15) Daily determine, God has given me a lot. How can I give back to Him? His word says if I give to Him, "He will open the floodgates of heaven and pour out so much blessing that I will not have room enough for it," (Malachi 3:10). That is living in the plus. Daily I determine I will do all that is possible to take care of my mind, my body and my spirit.

Daily I determine I will do all that is possible to take care of my mind, my body and my spirit.

Don't cloud up your mind with negative thoughts. Don't destroy your body with laziness and bad habits. Don't allow things to get between you and a positive relationship with God the Father. This challenge is for me and it's a challenge to you to live above the negative. This challenge is for us to take hold of God and live above zero balance and live life with a plus.

John 15:5, "I am the vine; you are the branches. If a man remains in me and I in him, he will bear much fruit; apart from me you can do nothing."

Dear friend. Are you trying to do life without Him? You'll live on empty. Your life will never be full. Will you trust in Him and remain in Him and allow Jesus to dwell in your life? He will fill the deepest needs of your heart.

CHAPTER NINE
REFLECTION AND MEDITATION

1. Sometimes life falls into the negative. What aspects of your life lately have been below zero?

2. When you run out of fuel, you are going to crash. Is there some area of life where you have crashed?

3. Jesus taught in John chapter 15 the vital importance of obeying His commands. Obedience to God is a decision to live life in the plus.

CHAPTER TEN

Making the Most of What is Left of Your Life

You feel a pain. You go see your doctor. He runs some tests. He says, "I have bad news. All evidence indicates you have 30 days to live." He tells you, "Whatever you need to do, you have thirty days in which to do it."

What are you going to do? What can you do in thirty days? First consider what you are not going to do:

Buy life insurance.

The insurance company will investigate. They will obtain your medical records and determine that you do not qualify for coverage.

Learn to play the piano.

If you have always said, "Someday I'm going to set aside the time and learn to play the piano. It's too late now.

Work your way up the corporate ladder. Even with great success it's not going to happen in a month.

Get in good physical condition. It takes more than a month to get in really good shape.

Build your retirement. Retirement income is developed over a number of many, many years of saving.

Become a good student. Report cards normally come out every six weeks. Therefore there is not enough time for you to show improvement.

Become a good Father or Mother.

Become a good husband or wife.

Obtain the college or graduate degree you've always wanted.

Make up for a wasted life.

What can you do in thirty days?

Update your will. Do you have a will? You can do this in just a little bit of time. Make sure that you leave something to the Lord's work. You cannot take it with you. It will be a great testimony to everybody who knows that you cared enough about the church or God's work to leave something to keep your church going after you are with God.

Close out some unfinished business. Pay off a bill. Or max out your credit cards if you choose, but it might not set well with whoever becomes the executor of your estate.

You can visit some family members if you are physically able.

Make your funeral arrangements. Buy a cemetery plot if you don't have one. Write out your funeral arrangements. Hire mourners. Write down what songs you want sung. Do you want to be cremated, buried in a mausoleum or in the ground?

Have a talk with your children or other close family members. In your case it might be your parents or a brother or sister. There is so much we never talk about. In the average home the only thing that is said is, "Turn that light out. Turn the music down. Be at home at midnight. No you are not wearing that to church. Dad do you have any money?"

Spend some time doing your favorite hobby.

Walk or drive your favorite road. I have several roads in East Kentucky that I ran as a teenager. There is an eleven-mile stretch between Frankfort Kentucky and Versailles that is beautiful horse country that I love to jog.

Repent of your sins and trust in Christ as your savior. It is never too late. However, if you wait until you have your death notice you are pushing your luck.

Follow Christ in baptism.

Join a church and in the last few days of your life become a spokes person for Jesus Christ. Jesus said, "As long as it is day, we must do the work of him who sent me. Night is coming, when no one can work," (John 9:4).

Romans 14:8, "If we live, we live to the Lord; and if we die, we die to the Lord. So, whether we live or die, we belong to the Lord."

Psalm 90:12, "So teach *us* to number our days aright, that we may gain a heart of wisdom."

James 4:14–15, "You do not even know what will happen tomorrow. What is your life? You are a mist that appears for a little while and then vanishes. Instead, you ought to say, 'If it is the Lord's will, we will live and do this or that.'"

In Luke 2:49 Jesus said, "I must be about my Father's business."

If we are going to make the most of what is left of our life we can find no better person to pattern our lives after than the Lord Jesus.

Notice carefully four qualities of His life that we must adapt to ours.

The Mission of His Life

Jesus had a mission. He once said, "For the Son of Man came to seek and to save what was lost," (Luke 19:10). The mission of Christ was about people. He came for a cross. He knew that He would die and that He would die for you. Do you ever wonder if somebody cares about you? Go to the Bible and there you will read about someone who cared about you so much that He went through a lot of abuse and death on a cross that you might have a reason to live.

So many people today feel hopeless and with almost no purpose or mission to their life. Five million people will attempt suicide in the United States this year alone. A person who commits suicide feels life for them is over and they cannot live here any longer.

My first cousin Harvey committed suicide. He was the world's greatest eighth grade basketball player. He scored over forty points a game in his eighth grade. I'm talking about twenty-five or more games. He married a beautiful girl after high school and had children. But his wife left him and it devastated Harvey so much that he could not cope with life. A couple of days before he killed himself he asked his mother, "If something happens to me will you take care of my daughter?" And of course she said she would, not thinking of what was to come. He went out from the house, close to a barn and shot himself. He had so much to live for. He was such a charismatic, personable kind of guy. He could have been anything he wanted to be. But he was without a mission.

Write out a mission statement for your life. If you do not already have one take some time and write out what your mission for the rest of your life is going to be. And then when the dark days come, you can go back and check your mission statement and likely you will have a reason to plow through the dark periods of life.

My mission statement in the last year or so of my life has become, "Trusting God everyday and doing the best I can with what I have."

Think about it. If somebody asks you what your mission in life is, what are you going to say? We hear this so much about churches. We hear about it for organizations but what about your life? If anything needs a mission it's human life. There is so much unguided and too often misdirected life in society today.

Maybe your mission is to make your wife happy or your husband happy. Maybe it's just to raise your children but then what? At every stage of life, young or old, we need a purpose for our existence.

The Motives of His Life

Jesus was motivated by His love for people. He redeemed people. He lifted them from despair. He encouraged others. He always brought a lift to discouraged lives. The community hated Zacchaeus, a tax collector. Tax collectors in that day and time were notorious for taxing people too heavily because that is how they made their living. The excess money the collectors charged was kept in their own pockets. But Jesus made such a difference when He visited Zacchaeus' home that Zacchaeus gave half of his possessions away to the poor and repaid those he had wrongly stole from four times the amount. When somebody makes that kind of change his or her heart has had a tremendous lift.

Jesus did it so many ways. He fed people, healed people, laughed with people, and went to parties and dinners. I think Jesus had such a great time. And that is also why the religious people of that day hated him so much. They thought Jesus was blasphemous because He associated with the notorious tax collectors and sinners of that day and time. But Jesus had a love for those who needed a lift in life and every one who gave Jesus a chance got a lift up in the right direction.

The Meaning of His Life

Jesus had something meaningful to do. What do you do? How many times in your life have you been asked that question? What do you do? We are so identified in life by what we do.

When I was a child I went through a very brief stage when I was embarrassed that my daddy was a coal miner. And then I started to look around and half of my friends didn't even have a daddy. An elderly grandparent or a single mom was raising them or their dads were on welfare. Then my attitude changed. It changed because I had a daddy period. I had friends and you do, too, that don't have a daddy around much or at all. Plus my father had something to do. He worked; and when he came home, we all worked some more. We had a large garden and livestock; and there were barns to clean out, and so many chores to do. There was always something to do.

What do you do? Jesus had something to do. In His younger life He was a carpenter and likely perfected this trade from His father. I doubt that Jesus had a lot of idle time as a kid. I suspect He worked hard; He was obviously an incredible student of Jewish teachings. In Luke chapter two, His mother and father found Him in the temple courts and He was sitting among the teachers listening and asking questions. "Everyone who heard him was amazed at his understanding and his answers." And then in Luke 2:52, "And Jesus grew in wisdom and stature, and in favor with God and men."

Someone has said for life to be meaningful we must have something to do, someone to love and something to look forward to. Does your life have meaning? Do you have something meaningful to do about your life?

Don't say you don't. I say you do. In Christ there is never a day that goes by that you can't help give someone a boost. There are plenty of people around to love. The majority of the people you are around each day are unsure if anybody in the world cares anything about them.

In Christ there is always something to look forward to.

In Christ there is always something to look forward to. Every day that we are in this world, even if it might be a few days, is a new day of opportunity and challenge. When this life ceases we are promised a better place with God in eternity.

The Moments of His Life

He only lived to be thirty-three, but think of His great moments. Notice just in the last three years of His life. He had a marvelous baptism. He was tempted by Satan himself in the wilderness for forty days but came through unscathed. On one occasion He fed over five thousand people. Once there was a funeral procession coming through town and this poor widow was broken hearted over her son's death and Jesus interrupted the procession and brought the boy back to life. Do you suspect that gave the little community of Nain anything to talk about? Whether it was The Sermon on the Mount or the Last Supper in an upper room or His death on a cross and resurrection from the grave, His life was filled with tremendous moments.

Do you sometimes think about your past . . . the many moments of the past—some blissful and others not so great? Life is that way; filled with one moment after another moment. And today good or bad is one of them. But if you knew you only had thirty days of life, what would you do with the rest of your life? How would you make the most of what is left of your life? And for some, you may not have that long.

> *If you knew you only had thirty days of life, what would you do with the rest of your life?*

My buddy Dennis was such a likeable guy. But after our senior year of school, he took a midnight swim in a friend's small lake and drowned. We couldn't believe it. Our senior class was distraught.

We had a good deacon's meeting one Sunday afternoon at the Stamping Ground Baptist Church. Scottie was a forty-year-old business owner. He went home after the deacon's meeting and decided he would take a quick nap before coming back to church. He told his wife, "Be sure you wake me. I want to go back tonight. But she couldn't wake him and she called me saying, "Glenn, Scottie's gone."

Our lives are a vapor. We are here a brief moment and then forever gone from this world. We number our days so that we might live wise. How many days do you have left? Maybe you have twenty years. Maybe you have thirty days. And if you have, I've given you a list of what you can do in thirty days. But maybe this is your last day.

If this is the last day of your life do you have some things you need to do? A call you need to make? Some prayers you need to pray?

It has been said many times, Plan out your life like you will live to be a hundred years old. But live each day like it's your last.

I challenge you to seize hold of your life and live it to the fullest and to do everything that you know that you should do and do it with all the strength that you have.

And if you are not ready to die, then you aren't ready to fully live for thirty more days. But if you know where you are going to be in eternity then you can fully and freely proceed with making the most of what is left of your life.

CHAPTER TEN
REFLECTION AND MEDITATION

1. What are some things you cannot do with only thirty days of life?

2. What can you do with only thirty days of life?

3. What are the four qualities of Jesus' life that we must adapt to ours?

CHAPTER ELEVEN

Be Wise and Use Common Sense

Ecclesiastes 10

Verse 1, "As dead flies give perfume a bad smell, so a little folly outweighs wisdom and honor." Error stands out—is bold. We seem to see error easier. All the buttons buttoned on the jacket except one will stand out. You can have your windshield spotless but if you have one dirty spot then all the attention is on that spot. We can do well all day to someone but if we say something hateful or wrong—that is what will be remembered.

Verse 2, "The heart of the wise inclines to the right, but the heart of the fool to the left." The wise man does the right thing. Sometimes it may not be what you want to do. We don't always want to do the right thing—like saying to someone, "I'm sorry," or make an effort to get along with a coworker that we really don't like.

Verse 3, "Even as he walks along the road, the fool lacks sense and shows everyone how stupid he is." How can you do that? You are driving down the road and here comes this guy walking toward you and you say, "Now that guy looks like a fool." Solomon is talking about discernment. Obviously a judgment such as this may not always be based on our sufficient information about that person. If a person is driving recklessly down the highway and endangering someone, then one's character is more displayed openly for scrutiny. Of if a person is acting in a way that is unkind or inconsiderate of others then he or she is displaying openly a character that opens them to criticism.

Verse 4, "If a ruler's anger rises against you, do not leave your post; calmness can lay great errors to rest." Don't get in a shouting match with your employer. Don't argue—just be quiet and do your work. There is a time to talk and a time to be quiet. The tongue can cause much trouble.

Verse 6, "Fools are put in many high positions, while the rich occupy the low ones. I have seen slaves on horseback, while princes go on foot like slaves." Jesus was not only the prince of peace—but also a servant. He helped others. He bowed His knee before His own disciples and washed their feet.

"Your attitude should be the same as that of Christ Jesus: Who, being in very nature God, did not consider equality with God something to be grasped, but made himself nothing, taking the very nature of a servant, being made in human likeness. And being found in appearance as a man, he humbled himself and became obedient to death—even death on a cross! Therefore God exalted him to the highest place and gave him the name that is above every name, that at the name of Jesus every knee should bow, in heaven and on earth and under the earth, and every tongue confess Jesus that Jesus Christ is Lord, to the glory of the Father." (Philippians 2:5-11)

"Whoever digs a pit may fall into it; whoever breaks through a wall may be bitten by a snake. Whoever quarries stones may be injured by them; whoever splits logs may be endangered by them. If the ax is dull and its edge unsharpened, more strength is needed but skill will bring success. (Ecclesiastes 10: 8 – 10) There is risk with almost everything we do. When we go out of the house each morning there is always some possibility of an accident. However, life cannot be lived in fear or we would not live life at all.

Verse 10, "If the ax is dull and its edge unsharpened, more strength is needed but skill will bring success."
In other words this verse is saying, work smarter—not harder. Here is a guy with a dull axe and he is really working hard—but achieving nothing. But a guy with a sharp axe accomplishes more with less effort because he has sharpened the blade.

Verse 11 "If a snake bites before it is charmed, there is no profit for the charmer." In other words, an ounce of prevention is worth a pound of cure."

Verses 12 – 13 talks about fools. "Words from a wise man's mouth are gracious, but a fool is consumed by his own lips. At the beginning his words are folly; at the end they are wicked madness." A fool's speech can bring him to ruin. A fool, he thinks, knows all. Have you ever met anybody that knew everything?

Verses 15–18, warn about laziness. "A fool's work wearies him; he does not know the way to town." And then in verse 18 we read, "If a man is lazy, the rafters sag; if his hands are idle, the house leaks."

Verse 20, "Do not revile the king even in your thoughts, or curse the rich in your bedroom, because a bird of the air may carry your words, and a bird on the wing may report what you say."

Everything gets repeated—everything you say is repeated. So again He warns about the use of the tongue, using common sense and applying wisdom. Notice it is a bird. A bad word about anybody usually has wings attached to it. Now if I brag about you it may eventually reach you or may never. Good words go around on a turtle, very slowly . . . but the negative has wings.

> *Some crops are slow but there is the principle of reaping what we sow. Most good crops take time and cultivation.*

Verse 1 of chapter 11, "Cast your bread upon waters, for after many days you will find it again. Give portions to seven, yes to eight, for you do not know what disaster may come upon the land."

In other words . . . some crops are slow but there is the principle of reaping what we sow. Most good crops take time and cultivation. Quality in any form seldom comes quickly. Say good words. Do good deeds. Help others. Be generous. Ask God for wisdom and common sense.

CHAPTER ELEVEN
REFLECTION AND MEDITATION

1. Error is bold. What errors do you have trouble erasing?

2. Do you argue? There is a time to talk and a time to keep quiet.

3. Life is filled with risks. What are some risks you take every day?

4. Ecclesiastes chapter ten is filled with common sense. What are some of the every day truths that you found in this chapter?

CHAPTER TWELVE

Life's Places

We read about places in the Bible. Jesus said, in John 14:2 to His disciples, "I am going to prepare a place for you," (And that will be a great place.)

"God is your refuge." (Deut. 33:27)

"You are my hiding place." (Psalm 32:7)

Matthew 27:33, "A place called Golgotha."

Everybody is some place while in this world. You may live in any state or other part of the world. You may live in an apartment or some large house. You may live in the country or inner city. Places are where people are located briefly. No one in this life is any place for a fixed time. Nothing is fixed forever on planet earth.

Some people may work twenty years to achieve a retirement home or place to reside but it's only for another twenty years of life at best.

Where are you in this life? What place are you in? Are you in a good place? Are you between a rock and a hard place? Are you in a happy place? Are you in a sad place? Are you in the very place you want to be? Or, would you like to escape your place?

Places We Choose to Be

We make a lot of choices throughout life. We may choose a fine restaurant. We may choose a special night out with the wife, family or best friend. Or it might be driving over to make a visit to your parents or visiting a son or daughter.

You may choose to take a walk, a swim or ride your bike. You might choose to sleep the day away or to work an extra shift at work. You may choose to change jobs or give your current work your very best effort and stay with it for the long haul. We may choose to strive for perfection or choose to foul up.

Places We Have to Be

We have a choice—but we know we have to be there. It may be those days when you don't feel like being at work but you go anyway. It may be a trip to the mall. You don't want to go but you know you promised your wife or your kids. So you do it.

It may be going to the funeral home. You have a choice. But we know the family and we know it's only right that we go out of respect. Meetings can be dull and boring but it may be related to work, children's education or church. Therefore, we go even though it may be mundane.

Places We Do Not Want to Be

How much of our lives do we spend in places we don't want to be . . . doing things we don't want to do?

Often we are with people that we don't want to be with. Sometimes we end up in these places because we chose to. We felt like we had to be there but we did not want to be. That is a terrible feeling. Have you ever chosen to be some place that you didn't want to be? And you thought to yourself, "I am here but I don't want to be here."

> *How much of our lives do we spend in places we don't want to be . . . doing things we don't want to do?*

"I'm at the mall, but I don't want to be at the mall; but my wife insisted I come."

The Israelites chose to enter into the wilderness, because they wanted to escape Egypt. But they did not want to stay in the wilderness near as long as they did. But why did they? The Israelites were constantly disobedient to God.

Sin and disobedience to God kept them in a place where they did not want to be, doing things they did not want to do . . . living in a way they did not desire to live. They desired the lush, plush land of Canaan. But they dwelled in the barren, unpleasant desert. And it took them 40 years to get out. It took them 40 years to catch on that all they had to do to have every thing they wanted and needed . . . to realize their potential . . . to achieve their goals was to love God and obey Him and have right hearts.

A couple of weeks ago, a man gave me this testimony. "He said "It's been amazing how much things in my life have turned upward since I began to get my heart and my life right with God. Family is better. Business is better. Life is better!"

The wilderness was a place they had to go to, but it wasn't a place they had to stay.

Don't you want that for you? There aren't any guarantees that your bottom line will double and that you are never going to have any problems . . . but when the Hebrews obeyed God and they got their lives in order with God they began to go in the upward more positive direction.

The wilderness was a place they had to go to, but it wasn't a place they had to stay. Are you in the wilderness? Are you there because of a choice? Are you there because of disobedience to God?

Jonah ended up in the wrong place. He wanted to go one way and God said no that's not what I had in mind. And Jonah therefore lived three days in a murky water hotel. It wasn't much of a vacation—definitely not a resort. A giant fish, the Bible says, swallowed him. It had to be scary.

Is life scary where you are? You go your own way, do your own thing, disobey God's word, live for sin and self and say, "Hah, I can get by with shaking my fist in God's face." No, life is just going to get scary for you. You see, you don't break God's commandments. You are broken when you willfully selfishly break God's word.

Adam and Eve knew firsthand what the Garden of Eden was like. It had to be good. But sin cost them the garden. And it put them in a place they never dreamed they would have to be and that was outside the garden.

Sin will take you farther than you want to go. It will keep you longer than you want to stay and it will cost you far more than you want to pay. "The wages of sin is death," (Romans 6:23).

Have you died? I know there were times when the Hebrews out in the wilderness thought, "We've died. We're just dead out here." When Jonah saw this giant fish coming he surely thought, "I'm dead." Are you like Adam and Eve? Have you lost the garden of your life? You don't live in the sunshine. You don't enjoy the forest for all the trees. You never hear the birds sing because you've lost the garden of your life.

Sin against God and disobedience to God while going your own selfish way is destructive. Thinking that you know more than everybody and that you know more than God will lead you to places you really don't want to be . . . keep you longer than you want to stay, and cost you far more than you want to pay.

God can save you from heartache. God led the Hebrews out of the desert and He can lead you out. God got Jonah out of the fish and He can get you out.

You know when things change in our lives? When our attitudes change. You go around with an attitude

"Hah I can play with fire and not get burned. I don't have to pay attention to God and His word." It will hurt you. But when you say . . . "I'm going to turn this ship around and turn it in the direction of the port of safety and happiness" . . . you will then begin to discover what Jesus said, "Come to me, all *you who are weary and burdened, and I will give you rest.*" (Matthew 11:28)

> *Sin and disobedience to God will give you sleepless nights, days of worry, and stress. Jesus offers rest, peace and joy.*

Sin, and disobedience to God will give you sleepless nights, days of worry, and stress. It will cast a dark shadow over your life. But Jesus offers rest, peace and joy. Sin takes all three of those away. Jesus, and a life and heart that are right with Him will offer this wonderful quality of life.

We don't always end up in places we don't want to be because of sin. Sometimes God is allowing us to be tested.

Daniel was in the Lion's den because there was none like him. You think he wanted to be there? No, that experience kept Daniel on his face before God all night. My wife Karen's favorite verse is " . . . weeping may remain for a night, but rejoicing comes in the morning," (Psalm 30:5). When they pulled Daniel out of that lion's den he surely thought . . . *Whew . . . glad it's morning.*

As Christians there are the dark times of life we have to endure and someday we are going to say, "Whew . . . it's morning!"

Do you think Shadrach, Meshach and Abednego wanted the fire? They were cast into a fiery furnace because they were devout in their faith. They didn't say, "Wow . . . this is such a cool place to be." No. They were in the fire, but God was there in the fire with them.

Here is a place. Matthew 27:33, "They came to a place called Golgotha." This is the place were they led Jesus to be crucified. Just the night before Jesus said, God if there is anyway you can get me out of this—I'm listening. But God did not get him out of it.

God did not take away the cross. Golgotha became the most hideous place in human history because there at that place they crucified Jesus. There at that place all your sins were paid for. At that place Jesus took your place on a cross. He died for us. And by the way, He died alone.

He is with us in the valley. He is with us in the fire—if we are with Him.

Jesus in that place went through hell so that you might not have to. Friend if you are living for Jesus, and your heart is right with God, you may be thrown into a fire of trial. But Jesus is with you in the fire. As I walk through the valley of the shadow of death you are with ME! He is with us in the valley. He is with us in the fire—if we are with Him.

Daniel and these three men chose to stick with God, and God stuck with them all the way. Don't you go around thinking "God is with me, God is with me . . . if you are living out of fellowship with Him. He's not. These men had power with God because they walked with Him.

Here is this guy driving down the Interstate at 90 mph. "God is with me," he says. No He's not, Jesus always gets out at 65. After 65 you're riding alone.

Job is a classic example. Job was a very godly man. God allowed Job to suffer and lose everything he had. Family, money, and health were all lost. Job never quit walking with God and in the end Job had more of all the three than he had ever had before. But, Job never wanted to be there. He never wanted to be in the place. He never asked for that position. And I would have been more like Job's wife than Job. I would have given God a good talking to.

I get irritated with God. I've heard my wife chew God out good. And I don't blame her as she has wrestled with multiple sclerosis for over eleven years.

The trials of life can make us discouraged . . . and tired. We can just give up and quit. Or our trials can make us angry and mad at God and mad at everybody.

"Let us not become weary in doing good, for at the proper time we will reap a harvest if we do not GIVE UP." (Galatians 6:9)

The building program of our church was a wilderness experience. Most massive projects are times of testing and trial. But as our church is obedient to God and we make Him first in our lives we will abound in people. There will be enough of everything that we need to be a shining lighthouse for Christ in our community.

Where do you choose to be? In the New Testament Jesus pictured a Pharisee and a sinner. The sinner or tax collector would not even, "look up to heaven, but beat his breast and said, 'God, have mercy on me a sinner." Jesus said, "I tell you that this man, rather than the other, went home justified before God," (Luke 18:13).

In the Bible the prodigal son chose to humble himself, admit that he had been wrong, and ask to be a servant in his dad's house. He turned and came home.

Joshua in the Old Testament said you serve who you want to serve. Live like you want to live but as for "Me and my house we will serve THE LORD," (Joshua 24:15).

The religious leaders told Peter and John . . . "Quit it, stop teaching and preaching in the name of Jesus." And they said, you can whip us. You can put us in jail. But there is one thing we cannot stop, and that is preaching, and singing and living for Jesus Christ." (Acts 4:19-20)

Would you . . . make that choice to live for Jesus? Would you today choose life over death? Will you choose heaven over hell? Peace over chaos or fulfillment over emptiness and joy over despair?

Life is often like a candy box with an assortment of choices.

CHAPTER TWELVE
REFLECTION AND MEDITATION

1. Where are you in life?

2. Are you happy? Why?

3. Where do you choose to be?

4. Where are places you have to be?

5. Life is filled with choices. What do you choose for today?

CHAPTER THIRTEEN

Prayer

"As for me, far be it from me that I should sin against the Lord by failing to pray for you." (1 Samuel 12:23)

Romans 1:9 and 10, "God, whom I serve with my whole heart in preaching the gospel of his Son, is my witness how constantly I remember you in my prayers at all times."

1 Thessalonians 5:17, "Pray continually."

Colossians 1:9,10 "For this reason, since the day we heard about you, we have not stopped praying for you and asking God to fill you with the knowledge of his will through all spiritual wisdom and understanding. And we pray this in order that you may live a life worthy of the Lord and may please him in every way."

Ephesians 1:15-16, "For this reason, ever since I heard about your faith in the Lord Jesus and your love for all the saints, I have not stopped giving thanks for you in my prayers."

Psalm 116:2, "Because he turned his ear to me, I will call on him as long as I live."

Acts 6:4, "and will give our attention to prayer and the ministry of the word."

Psalm 40:1, "I waited patiently for the Lord; he turned to me and heard my cry."

Proverbs 3:6, "In all your ways acknowledge him and he will make your paths straight."

Psalm 145:18, "The Lord is near to all who call on him."

What do you pray about? Who do you pray for? I think I normally try to request prayer for my wife, my father and mother, my children, myself.

Somebody said one time that I was the first pastor the church had ever prayed for. What they meant was that I was the first pastor of the church who had obvious need for prayer. My invalid wife kept much of my Christian family in prayer for me. The fact that Christian people pray for me helps my family and me.

Once I asked, "What if my wife weren't sick and she were able to jump off the swimming pool diving board and run marathon races. Would you still pray for me?"

I think we often limit our prayers. We pray for the sick and the needy and the downtrodden. But doesn't everybody need prayer?

What if most of the healthiest members in the average church gathering said, "Pray for me." Would we look at that person and wonder, "What's wrong with him/her?" Why would we hesitate to say, "Pray for me"? Is a request for prayer an admittance of weakness? Is a request for prayer for our family or us a declaration of need or problems?

Unfortunately that is when we often call unto God. "Lord the plane is crashing save me." Or Lord I'm going under rescue me." Prayer is to be daily. Prayer is talking to God.

When you say, pray for me. You are saying . . . talk to Father about me. Mention my name to Dad. Lift me up to the Father.

Who does not need or want to be remembered before the Father? Don't we all need Him? Don't you need God everyday? And don't we all need His mercies and guidance and wisdom?

> *When you say, pray for me. You are saying . . . talk to Father about me. Mention my name to Dad. Lift me up to the Father.*

We often have many unspoken requests. Why are they unspoken? They are because sometimes they are for good reason. We are praying about something that is nobody else's business.

You've heard the story about the three clergymen. A Methodist, a Presbyterian and a Baptist. One said, "I want you to pray for me because I have a problem with alcohol. I am confiding this to you in prayer. Please join with me in prayer about this." The Presbyterian said, "I have a real problem with womanizing and infidelity but I'm glad I have you men to pray for me and I'm glad I have you two to confide this in. And the Baptist said, I need your prayers too because I have a serious problem with gossip . . . and I can't wait to tell everybody what you two have been doing."

Is this why we have so many unspoken requests? Are they unspoken because we just don't want everybody to know . . . and it's not anybody else's business? Or do we not want to admit that we need prayer?

My problems are obviously highlighted and known because everybody knows of my wife's illness. But what if everybody in church or Christian assemblies instead of offering an unspoken request really poured their heart out and said, "This is something that I can't handle and I need for you to lift me up in prayer"?

A friend said that if every person honestly revealed what he or she was requesting prayer about, that it would be scary. Well, maybe. But maybe it would break the church into a spirit of real revival. It's difficult to have a burden or concern if we don't know what to have a burden about.

It's not my brother or my sister, but it's me Lord, standing in the need of prayer. Regardless if you are broken down with disease, or sin or grief or if someone has just given you five million dollars, we need prayer and need to be lifted up to the Father.

Life is like chocolate. Select prayer every day. Even at this very moment you can lay this book down and go to the Father in prayer. Prayer is a delight and a lift to every life and heart.

CHAPTER THIRTEEN
REFLECTION AND MEDITATION

1. What does the Bible say about prayer?

2. What are your prayer requests for today?

3. When do we pray the most? What is your unspoken prayer request?

4. Why are you afraid to share this prayer request with a prayer partner?

5. Select prayer every day.

CHAPTER FOURTEEN

Significance of the Present
A Matter of Perspective

I consider that our present sufferings are not worth comparing with the glory that will be revealed in us." (Romans 8:18)

I'm only about seven or eight years older than my two sister's sons. And when I was about ten years old I was still playing cowboy and Indians and had a fine arsenal of toy guns, rifles and other kinds of artillery necessary for fighting bad guys.

My nephew Randall was at my house one Saturday night and this little aggravating nephew broke my 30/30 toy rifle. It infuriated me so bad that I went into a rampage. I screamed and hollered and cried. I locked myself in the bathroom and wouldn't have anything to do with my sister until she got that little brat out of the house. It was really a big deal you know. Here was my $1.99 toy gun demolished. It seemed like a big deal then. But you know today when I think about that toy 30/30 rifle I don't scream or kick the floor or cry. I just kind of smile and think, "How insignificant."

Has anything like that ever happened to you? Maybe it was something you experienced as a child but now it's maybe 20 years later and all the agony you went through as a child doesn't seem so bad right now. I remember having my appendix removed when I was about eight or nine years old. My dad had to carry me out to the car. I was so sore and my side was hurting so bad that I couldn't walk. And it was scary. Today I remember that it was just one of those events along the road of life. And while it seemed so big then it's not such a big deal now.

Sometimes we go through things that we never seemingly get over. Losing a toy gun is one thing. But there is one lady whose daddy sexually molested her as a child and it's taken her years of counseling just to try to deal with it. Maybe now she has worked through it but there is an emotional ache that still exists in her life.

When I was a pastor of a church close to Cincinnati, we had this debate among some of the members over a stained glass window. On Sunday mornings the sun would literally blind half the congregation. About half the people wanted to cover it with some kind of blind or curtain but the other half didn't. There was this big business meeting over the blind and several people got all jerked out of shape because they didn't want it covered. So often appearance and vanity win out over substance. Now 20 years later, all of that disruption is a distant memory.

When I was a junior in high school I had this really bad car wreck and spent two weeks in the hospital. I was crushed because my year at school was really messed up. But we had this really good looking blonde cheerleader that I never dated but we were friends and she would come and push me around in my wheelchair and that really eased the pain.

While that two-week hospital stay at the time seemed eternal, and being knocked out of playing basketball most of my junior year was painful, in the whole scheme of things it was quite a learning experience. And it helped me then to see some things that were important and others that weren't so important.

It seemed like it took forever for our children to be born. Pregnancy just seemed to last forever. I don't know how it felt to my wife but it seemed like a long time to me. Now my sons are growing up and they are as big or bigger than I. And while pregnancy or diapers or those early years seemed like they would last forever, they're gone and are now only pleasant memories.

When I was 18 I thought it would be just the biggest deal to get away from home and go to college and be on my own. And I like you, enjoy independence. But then I had to do my own laundry and nobody did my laundry like my mother. My mother folded my clothes like nobody. She ironed and neatly folded all my underwear. Hey how about you? Do you iron your underwear? My mom ironed mine. Now when I married, it was a shock to me to find out that not everybody irons their underwear and if I liked mine that way I would have plenty of opportunities to practice doing it . . . for the rest of my life. And so my perspective changed to realize that I could survive by just getting them out of the dryer and putting them on.

Has your perspective ever changed about anything? Did you ever feel strongly about something and then after months or maybe even years you one day began to change your opinion? Have you ever had a preconceived notion about somebody and then found out you were totally wrong? You thought here is somebody that is a real bad guy or jerk but then you got to know the person and found out (he really is a jerk) or he's a nice guy or maybe you found out just the opposite.

Consider, the insignificant things of life. I can't determine that for you. I can't say what will be insignificant for you at the end of life. For me, my nephew breaking a toy gun doesn't amount to anything today. But that was a long time ago.

A loss in the final regional championship in 1973 was bone crushing. One of my best friends and I wept all the way out of the locker room. But you know after 27 years now I can look back at that and say, "Yes it would have been nice to have won . . . but it was just a ballgame and we didn't play up to our potential or we would have won."

Of course when you win it is different. And if we want to talk about the championship game of the district tournament where we won . . . now that's another story. We smile a little longer and it's always more fun remembering the victories of life. But we have to ask in the whole scheme of things what does it really matter? The only people that remember that game are those of us who won.

When I was a young 16 year old baby Christian I heard a woman come to church one night and in the middle of a business meeting stood and just started saying a lot of bad things about one of the other members. At the time it was scary. I thought the devil sure is here tonight and right there he stood. But the church had a lot of wise members in it that handled the situation carefully and the church and life went on. Looking back now it wasn't that much of a major issue. But it was sad that someone had that much hate in them and released it on a brother at church.

Somebody was giving me a hard time once because they heard the building committee wasn't putting carpet under the pews in our new building. A couple of weeks later they came back and said, "I was kind of silly to have gotten so upset. Quite honestly what the committee did looks good. In the whole scheme of things it really isn't that big of a deal."

What are those things that you have been upset over? And truthfully when your life is near its end and you look back, it really will not have been all that important what you got worked up over.

How many times have you gotten angry over something and a 100 years from now who will care? Maybe it wasn't so insignificant. Maybe it was very significant. Maybe somebody you really loved got hurt.

And you had to really put it in the hands of God to cope with it. And while 25 years has eased the pain you still bear the scar.

Over twelve years ago when Karen and I lost a little baby our world crashed. While there was nothing about that event that was insignificant, time brings healing. We look back now at that with not as much pain. We praise God for the wonderful children we have. We must believe that the child we lost will realize his full potential in heaven. When we think about heaven and how long heaven is going to be and how short life is and how great heaven is going to be. Our perspective has to change.

J.T. and Annabelle Ryan were friends of ours who lost a little baby in a fire. Their house caught fire one night and they didn't get the baby out. When I first met J.T and Annabelle they were already about 70 years old. And seldom did I ever see either of them when they didn't have a smile and a very positive outlook on life. So one day I asked Annabelle, "Mrs. Ryan how have you survived losing your child in that fire? She replied, "For many years it was devastating. But I had to realize all my grief and guilt for being unable to save him was killing me. I've lived my life without that child. But I won't live eternity without him."

She knew she would see that child again in heaven. And the closer she got to heaven the happier Annabelle seemed to get.

Paul said in 1 Corinthians 13:11-12, "When I was a child, I talked like a child, I thought like a child, I reasoned like a child. When I became a man, I put childish ways behind me. Now we see but a poor reflection as a mirror; then we shall see face to face. Now I know in part; then I shall know fully, even as I am fully known."

There is so much of this life we don't understand but someday we will. I can't imagine ever in this world ever feeling anything positive about my wife's illness. But let's say Karen is sick for another ten years and dies . . . what difference will that make in eternity? Possibly the first few days in heaven it will still bother me. I don't know, but there's no sorrow in heaven. The Bible says God will wipe away the tears from our eyes. I think that really means when we get to heaven it's going to be so awesome that we're going to look back on life and this world like we did all the home work we did or do in school and say, "Life . . . oh yeah, big deal . . . wow look at all this."

> *There is so much of this life we don't understand but someday we will.*

How are we going to view the diseases of this life after we've been in heaven ten thousand years? I think we will view this life after being in heaven like I view the loss of a toy gun as a child.

"When we've been there ten thousand years bright shining as the sun, we've no less days to sing God's praise than when we first begun."[4]

"Yes I had cancer but look where I am now. Yes life was tough, but look now."

Romans 8:18, "I consider that our present sufferings are not worth comparing with the glory that will be revealed in us."

And while there is so much that may seem so significant at the moment—in comparison to all of life and eternity . . . there is so much that will someday seem insignificant.

What about the Significant Things of life?

Significant Words

People have a hard time forgetting what you say. If you don't believe it, the Bible says "men will have to give account on the day of judgment of every careless word they have spoken," (Matthew 12:36). I'm not sure that I understand this verse. But I think it at least underscores the weight of our words. Notice the Bible says, *careless.* How do you talk to people? Have you told anybody off lately? What you might say about somebody is certainly always significant.

Significant Acts of Kindness

A girl was talking about her mother dumping her and

---

[4] *Amazing Grace! How Sweet the Sound*, The Baptist Hymnal 330.

her father and running off with another man. She said, "Glenn my daddy was so good to me." We have trouble forgetting how people make us feel—if you embarrass somebody or hurt somebody, it has a lasting impact.

Significant Decisions

There is the decision about YOU and how you live your life. We all make decisions about our lives. But there are three decisions that will affect our lives.

Education and training have a life long impact. What you study to do and become will impact your future. You cannot become what you do not prepare yourself for.

I cannot be a surgeon. However, training can begin at about any stage of life if you live long enough. I have a 41-year-old friend who taught school for 15 plus years and then decided he wanted to be physician but he had to go back to school and now he's in his residency program.

You cannot become what you do not prepare yourself for.

Who you marry will have a life long impact—whether you divorce or stay together. Your life is altered for the better or worse depending on whom you marry. Sometimes your life is made richer or sometimes it's made for better or it's made for poorer or worse.

A word to teenagers is—be careful whom you get emotionally involved with because you could end up going way too far and it will effect the course of your life forever. Marriage under great circumstances takes a lot of work and there is stress under the best of circumstances.

You can be friends with a lot of people but choose carefully whom you give your heart to. I counsel teenagers to make dating casual. You will discover a sense of freedom if you are just going to the ballgame or the movie with a friend. There's none of this physical pressure and you have the freedom to just be yourself and to enjoy life. Somewhere along the line you'll make a good friend that you may decide you want to spend your life with. Tragically many couples never find out if they are friends until they are ready for a divorce.

Your life is altered for the better or worse depending on whom you marry.

I want to say with everything that I have been through the many years of my life with my wife—if God had showed it to me on videotape before our marriage it would have terrified me. Unquestionably, it would have not changed my decision.

I ask young adults to think about that. If this person you are about to marry should become so sick that they could not feed themselves, bathe themselves, take themselves to the bathroom, would you still marry that person? If you cannot answer that question emphatically yes—if you have some doubt, then don't do it. Because there is a likely chance that you will be in that position. Don't think your marriage is always going to be passionate love and romance. The body fails and changes and so the circumstances change.

The third decision and most important is about Christ. Our decision about Christ is the most important decision we will ever make. My pastor said that the three greatest decisions we make in life is our career choice, our marriage choice, and our decision about Christ; and that everything else about our lives is affected by these three choices.

> *Our decision about Christ is the most important decision we will ever make.*

But our jobs and whom we marry are affected by our decision for Christ. At the end of our lives our career won't take us to heaven. Our marriage won't take us to heaven. When we face the hour of sickness, Jesus is the great physician. When we face the hour of uncertainty, Jesus is the gentle shepherd who leads us. Even when we walk through the valley of the shadow of death, He is with us. When we face the hour of grief, Jesus knows how we feel. And He understands.

When we are lonely, we are never alone because He is the Friend that sticks closer to us than a brother. And when we die He is the one who has promised us eternal life. When we've been there ten thousand years what is going to matter the most is not how many hours we spent at the office, how much money we made and left to our estate, not how many monuments where erected to our name.

What will matter is that there was a time in our lives when we made an eternal decision for Christ. If you have not trusted in Christ, Jesus died on the cross that you might live. What will really be significant 200 years from now? Where will your soul be one hundred years from now? The Bible says, "For God so loved the world that he gave his one and only son, that whoever believes in him shall not perish but have eternal life." (John 3:16) That promise means something today and it will mean something 100 years from now if you will claim this promise for yourself at this very moment.

CHAPTER FOURTEEN
REFLECTION AND MEDITATION

1. Recall an experience that seemed significant but now is insignificant.

2. Has your perspective changed about anything?

3. What is an event that is in the past but scarred you emotionally or physically?

4. How has God helped you to deal with that event and put it behind you?

5. What is really significant in life?

CHAPTER FIFTEEN

Selecting and Enjoying the Moment

Have you ever had a special moment? One that you never wanted to forget? Or maybe you've had moments you just as soon forget. It's those moments that touch us or affect us in special ways that etch a special place in our hearts.

You remember Moses going up to Mount Sinai where God gave him the Ten Commandments? They were so important that God etched them in stone. (Exodus 24:12) I want you to *remember* these commandments so they are written in *stone!* The people were watching what was going on. Chapter 20:18 says, "The people saw the thundering, and the lightening, and the noise of the trumpet, and the mountain smoking."

Have you ever watched a sporting event and maybe there was one player that could not do anything wrong? Every pass was complete, every shot was a made basket. Or maybe you've seen a runner flying by everyone on the one-hundred-yard dash. And we might say, wow that guy is smoking!

Well God was really working . . . God was smoking. This was an incredible moment between God and Moses.

When the Israelites crossed the Jordan in Joshua chapter 4, it was such an incredible moment. The Lord spoke to Joshua saying take for yourselves, twelve men from the people, one man from each tribe, and command them: take up for yourselves twelve stones from here out of the middle of the Jordan from the place where the priests' feet are standing firm, and carry them over with you and lay them down in the lodging place where you will lodge tonight.

1 Samuel 7:12, God had enabled Samuel to have a great victory against the Philistine army and the Bible says it was such a great moment in Samuel's life that "Samuel took a stone and set it up between Mizpah and Shen. He named it Ebenezer," (the stone of help) saying, "Thus far has the Lord helped us." This is an incredible time . . . what a moment.

In Mark 9:2 Peter, James, and John witnessed the transfiguration of Christ, and the scripture says it appeared Jesus was talking with Moses and Elijah. During this experience the Bible says there was a cloud that overshadowed them and a voice that came out of the cloud saying, this is my beloved Son: hear Him. Peter said, Lord, let's make three tabernacles, one for you, Moses and Elijah. This has been such a marvelous experience we don't want to forget this moment.

I completed my college degree at Georgetown in August 1977. I got to go through the graduation ceremony in May, but I had a semester of Greek I had to complete—*Greek.* When the postmaster handed me that envelope in August with that BA diploma, I felt a sense of victory.

Know the Moment

Count your blessings one by one. Peter realized this was a great moment. The Roman Soldier at the cross—I believe that he realized the moment.

Do you enjoy the moments of life? I took the ferry over to Martha's Vineyard back in August. It was a nice one-hour ride. I sat on the dock and looked at the sailboats and the beautiful blue sky and I said, "God thank you for this moment in my life."

Zach and I got off the new 3D ride based on the comic character Spider Man at Universal Studios and when we got off that ride we just laughed and said, "What a ride! That was *too cool!* Let's do it again! I thought to myself, what a moment.

Truthfully, it's just been the last year of my life that I have realized the value of moments. Jay and the Americans sang, "This Magic Moment." But I think we all have a lot of these moments in life. We just don't recognize them at the time. We see the flowers but we don't stop and smell them. The sun is shining and the sky is blue but we don't take notice.

Every time I kiss my wife, I pay close attention. Whenever I get exhausted while exercising and start laughing because I get this rush from a good work out, I think, God, this is great. Thank you.

Enjoy the Moment

Do you take the time to enjoy life? Samuel said, the Lord has helped us and been good to us. Let's stop and enjoy this moment. Peter said, this has been some experience; we need a memorial stone set up in remembrance of what happened here. We will never cross the Jordan River quite like this again. We need some memorial stones to commemorate this experience.

Do you enjoy your vanilla ice cream? Do you enjoy your walks in the sun? Do you enjoy your company with people? Where ever you are, be all there. Enjoy church. Enjoy the Bible and the people and the music and when you get into your car, enjoy your ride home.

Don't let good moments pass. We have Thanksgiving to stop and give thanks. We have Christmas to stop and celebrate the birth of Christ. We have birthdays and anniversaries to remember those special days.

What about people you see at church? Do you take a moment to say hi? Do you shake a few hands? Do you think of church as being special? The moments you share in church never are exactly repeated. They may seem the same every Sunday in many churches. But people come and go or go on to heaven and church is rarely ever quite the same forever.

I have some videotape of great moments in our family. Not near enough. I wish I had more. We got out some old videotape of Jared and Zachary when they were about seven and five years old. They were dancing in the family room and I mean they were getting with it. We watched that the other day and we just laughed and laughed about it.

Then we watched some tape of their mother singing beautifully and looking great, and it broke our hearts. I was glad we found that tape because it helped us to remember just how talented their mother was.

Now you can't pick up a moment, put it in your pocket and carry it with you forever, but you can take pictures and video. When a moment presents itself, act on it.

When Karen and I were on our first date, she didn't really want to be with me. Some friends of ours, Jim and Anne Falkenberg, had invited Karen to this pizza place and I was just supposed to be there. I don't think Karen liked it that I was there. When we were finished eating, Jim and Anne said, well we've got to go. Karen, you just ride home with Glenn . . . and she was stuck. We got into my car and I was taking her home. By the time we were getting close to her driveway I started my speech. "Look I know you aren't interested in me and I understand and I won't bother you anymore. So I took her by the hand and gave her hand a little kiss and she didn't turn loose of my hand. I had her. Six months later we were married. Karen later told me "When you kissed my hand, that's what did it." Well, what if I had let that moment pass?

There are obviously some moments in life that we need to let pass. Rethinking what we might say before we tell somebody off is one of them.

But sometimes we miss a lot of great moments in life simply because we let them pass. Saying a good word to somebody. Encouraging somebody. Helping someone out. Spending a moment talking and getting to know an individual.

> *Sometimes we miss a lot of great moments in life simply because we let them pass. Saying a good word to somebody. Encouraging somebody. Helping someone out.*

In Philippi, Acts 16, there once was an earthquake. A Philippian jailer knew at that moment he wanted to become a Christian and he didn't let the moment pass. He went to Paul and Silas and said, "What must I do to be saved?"

The Ethiopian Eunuch in Acts 8, and Phillip were walking and they came to some water. The Eunuch said, here is some water . . . what would keep me from being baptized? And Phillip said, do you believe in Jesus Christ? Then they went down at that very moment and Phillip baptized him.

Jesus was sitting in the house of Mary and Martha, and Mary gets an idea . . . hey . . . there is something I can do for Jesus. She goes and obtains the most precious expensive gift she has—her alabaster perfume and just pours it all over Jesus. Jesus took note of the moment. He said, what she has done will be remembered as a memorial to her. And here we are now remembering what Mary did. Mary didn't miss the moment to love Jesus. If she had waited . . . an hour or two . . . she might not have ever had that opportunity to love Jesus in that way. Mary had enough perception about her to act on that moment.

What does God say to you? What does God want you to do? Walk while you have the light . . . before the darkness comes. Opportunities come and go, but they don't stay around forever.

Oh the Moments We Miss

Paul, one time stood before King Agrippa and preached the gospel to him and the king said, Paul, this is an incredible moment! I'm almost persuaded to become a Christian! At this moment right now Paul you've really got me thinking. You have my interest stirred. I'm thinking this would be a good thing to respond to the call of God upon my life. But he never did. He never became a Christian. The road to hell is paved with what? Good intentions. Good *intentions.* I'll do it someday. I'll do it later. I'll do it tomorrow.

There was never a better moment in history for Agrippa to be saved, and he let it pass and probably died and went to hell.

At this very moment if there is something you need to do, you should do it. If you need to give your life to Christ you should. If you need to respond to what God is wanting for your life, you should respond.

CHAPTER FIFTEEN
REFLECTION AND MEDITATION

1. What has been the best moment of your life?

2. What are the special moments of life you reflect on often?

3. We have moments daily. How are we to respond to the moments of life?

CHAPTER SIXTEEN

The Power of Life!

On a couple of occasions I've tried the Low Carbohydrate Diet. I lost a few pounds but after a couple of weeks, I was so weak that I didn't feel like getting off the couch. That's not exactly what I wanted. I wanted to feel better and look a little better because I know enough about my body to know that when I am at a certain weight, and at a small level of sweets, that I have more zing in my life. I feel better, have a better outlook and am all around happier. And if I can choose to eat some foods and then not eat some other foods and have enough daily activity that makes me feel good then why wouldn't I want to do that?

How about you? Don't you feel better when you have some zip and zing to your life? When do you feel better and stronger? We don't always have those days, but we feel so much better when we do.

I like to feel good. I enjoy feeling healthy and strong. It's a feeling that is not forever because we are not immortal. Our bodies change but we should take care of them as long as we can.

Occasionally I have to make adjustments in my life. A writing pad works the very best for me. When I daily write down what I eat and how many calories I've burned off it helps me keep track of what the true story is.

I have some understanding of feeling good because I've seen human life feel so bad. I've been around enough people who because of sickness were just physically depleted of any energy or power in their living. And anybody that has ever felt good, knows that feeling bad is a lousy feeling. I think you would say I enjoy feeling good. I enjoy strength and power and zip in my life.

We like power in our bodies. We enjoy that zest and the zing of life. Let me ask you—how do you feel? Health changes; enjoy the health that you have today!

We enjoy power in our daily living. Much of our living is our work. If you are a student, it is school. Or much of your life may be the hours you spend making home an enjoyable experience for your family.

I love it when I can have a great productive day in God's word and feel like God has not only spoken to me but has given me something that I might share with others. Or when I've had the opportunity to have a conversation with somebody about Jesus and that conversation made a difference in their lives.

I know if you are a student you feel better about school when you've had a good day in class, when the teacher said well done or you felt like you really had a handle on your homework.

At the job you want to feel productive. You want to enjoy your work and your eight or more hours that you give each day. You want it to feel rewarding. And you want to do your best.

We enjoy power in our relationships. With the husband or wife we want to be able to say that we're just great together as a team in our marriage. Our marriage has a lot of power to it. We feel we are in a great relationship with our children when the conversation is really going well or we're doing something together. Or even in our friendships, it is wonderful to have open communication and fellowship.

We enjoy power with God. How great it is to feel and know we have some zip with God. When we pray, He hears us. When we walk, He is beside us. When we hurt, He hurts with us. When we face life, we have His comfort and help.

The main reason we don't have power or zip in our relationship with God is when we are dead. Dead bodies have no zip. A dead body is cold and lifeless. Why? Because the body is dead.

In the New Testament John chapter 11, Lazarus had been dead four days. There was no life or power in the body of Lazarus. He had no zest. No zip.

Have you ever seen a dead body? Do you remember the classic line from the movie sixth sense?

"I see dead people."

Bruce Willis asked, "Right now?"

And the kid replied, "All the time." We live in a world of dead people.

"For the wages of sin is death." (Romans 6:23) People fill the world but they are dead in sin. We hear a lot about people being arrested for making drugs. And usually it's some dilapidated house they show on television where they are making the drugs. They have kids that are hungry and don't have adequate clothing. You think, that's sad . . . people who are just dead; they have no life.

I talk to people in marriages where the relationship is dead. There is no conversation, very little time together if any, and the relationship has just died. And usually it happens in a subtle kind of way. No marriage starts out with the intent of dying along the way.

We don't start out in life with the intent of dying. The idea is to live. But somewhere along the way we allow ourselves to go into a deep sleep. We see this happen in churches. A church starts out with the vision of being the living breathing body of Christ but somewhere along the line either sleep or death sets in.

We live in a world of dead churches. To the church at Sardis, Jesus said, "I know your deeds; you have a reputation of being alive, but you are dead. Wake up!" (Revelation 3:1,2)

Walter McNeil was a dear friend and just a couple of days before Easter 1992. He was slipping away.

"Walter."

"Yes what is it?" He thought I was calling him back for something. For a few moments he aroused and then hours later he went on to be with the Lord.

Even the best of people and churches can get real sleepy. The Lord Jesus Christ says to us . . . "WAKE UP!" Come alive!

Jesus said to Lazarus in the tomb . . . "Lazarus come out of that tomb." That had to be something when a dead man arose from the grave and he still had those grave clothes on. Jesus was saying, "Lazarus come to life!" I want to challenge you now to come to life!

The Devil Has Two Major Tools

The first tool is discouragement. The devil wants you to be discouraged. If he can get you down and discouraged he has you beat.

Here is the boxer. It's the seventh round. He is bleeding. The eyes are swollen. He cannot lift his arms. He is so discouraged he says, "I quit. I'm beat. I'm dead." He's out of it.

Here is the marathoner. The race is on but he is into the 15th mile and here comes a big hill. His legs are beginning to hurt and his feet are aching tired. He is exhausted and the hill is so tough it breaks him down. He gets so discouraged that he can't go on. So he drops out of the race.

The devil was auctioning off some of his tools one day and someone said, "I'll buy that one."

But the devil said, "That one is not for sale. When nothing else works I use that one and win every time." Friend, has the devil got you discouraged? Are you beat down? Are you tired and bleeding and feeling like you don't have enough power to go on? Not enough strength to make the journey? Can't do it; you're whipped?

His second major tool is the lullaby. He wants to lull us to sleep. Now we all need rest; but there's a limit to that. When you are asleep you are inactive. There is not much going on when you are asleep. When you are asleep you are not telling others about Christ. When you are asleep you are very inactive.

The devil is a master violin player but he only plays one tune—go to sleep. The angel told John on the Isle of Patmos, tell that church at Sardis to wake up and come to life!

Is the devil trying to pull one of these two tricks at the place where you worship? Is he trying hard to discourage you or just lull you to sleep spiritually? You know what happens to us? Sometimes it just slips up on us.

In 2 Kings 6:1–7, Elisha and the prophets were cutting trees for a new building. While they were cutting trees, one of them lost an iron axe-head. It fell into the water and there was panic.

"Oh my Lord, he cried out, it was borrowed." Now by some miracle the axe-head floated back to the top of the water and the man reached his hand in and saved it. They weren't going to be cutting any trees without the axe-head. Why? Because there was no cutting edge. The axe-head gave them their sharpness to get the job done. It added a sense of life to their swings. Without it they could flail the day away; but with it, they had zip and life in their work. However, they lost their cutting edge in the *middle* of doing the work even though they were working *hard.*

I've seen people and churches work so hard for so long that suddenly one day the people and the church were overwhelmed with deadness. Is it possible to just lose your cutting edge right while you are doing the work? Is it possible to just get unenergized? We like to be like the energized bunny and keep going, but we're not built like that. And sometimes we get so very tired. Is it possible to become so discouraged that we either quit or die? The answer to these questions is yes. You can lose your zing. You can become powerless, weak and frail. "Remember what is right," said the angel to John in Revelation.

Do what is right. Do the truth. Do what you know that works. James 4:10, "Humble yourselves before the Lord, and he will lift you up."

"Resist the devil, and he will flee from you. Come near to God and he will come near to you." (James 4:7) Remember what you have received and heard. And obey it. Walk in the light that you have. Recall the truth that you have already learned and put it into action.

Repent. Turn from that which is making you ineffective. Turn away from those things that are not making you a better person or those things that come between you and your relationship with God. There are some activities and sins and lifestyle that kill the spirit and power of God working in your life. So, why continue? Why hold onto that which is robbing you of your power?

On that day when Lazarus came back to life, Jesus was the start and the source. He was the sustaining strength that brought life back to him. Without Jesus, Lazarus would have never come out of that tomb.

Jesus can bring you back to life today. He can give you your life back. He may not give back to you an ex marriage partner, a deceased child or spouse . . . not even likely an old job, and probably not even the body of your youth. But Ephesians 2:5 says "God, who is rich in mercy, made us alive with Christ even when we were dead in transgressions."

Jesus was the start and the source. He was the sustaining strength that brought life back to him. Without Jesus, Lazarus would have never come out of that tomb.

"I can do everything through him who gives me strength." (Philippians 4:13) He makes us alive. He strengthens us.

What did the father say about his son after he had been away so long, living in a hog pen, eating the hog's food? The son returned home and the father says, let's have a party! It's time for a big celebration. "For this my son was dead, and is alive again; he was lost and is found." (Luke 15:24)

Anytime a person wakes up, makes a change, gets things right with himself and with God, it's party time in heaven. I know I'm going to like heaven because I love parties.

That's the way it ought to be in church every time somebody comes to Christ or follows Christ in baptism. We ought to really celebrate and feel great.

God loves it when we wake up, come back to life and reclaim the power of living. How about you? Are you ready for some zip? Are you ready for some real power? Jesus Christ *is* your power. John 10:10, "I have come that they may have life, and have it to the full."

Are You Dead or Are You Alive?

Faith—you may need to reaffirm and recommit your faith in Christ. "If we confess our sins, he is faithful and just and will forgive us our sins and purify us from all unrighteousness," (1John 1:9).

Adjustment—it may be that before you can experience any power in your life that you have to make some major adjustments in your lifestyle, your prayer life and your attitude. Psalm 66:18, "If I cherished sin in my heart, the Lord would not have listened."

Obedience—John 14:23, "If anyone loves me, he will obey my teaching. My Father will love him, and we will come to him and make our home with him."

What might happen if you added power to your life? You will be changed as a person. You'll get up in the morning and seize the day. You'll have the energy to face the problems and storms that come your way. If you add power to your life you will be strengthened in every good relationship in your life and have the power to rid yourself of the bad ones. Your life will be changed—for the better!

CHAPTER SIXTEEN
REFLECTION AND MEDITATION

1. We enjoy power in life. Where are some areas we want power?

2. Why do we sometimes feel powerless with God?

3. What are two tools of the devil?

4. Sometimes we lose our cutting edge. How can we get our edge back?

CHAPTER SEVENTEEN

The Great Physician

The first time I became aware of any health deficiencies in my life was when I was about seven or eight years old. I had a continuing problem with tonsillitis. One time, my grandma placed my hands on the radio and we prayed together with Oral Roberts.

My parents sought out a physician and that physician removed my tonsils and tonsillitis became a thing of the past for me.

One day, years later my father would carry me out to our car because my side was so sore and hurting so bad that I couldn't walk. Dr. Bob Hall removed my appendix and within a week or so I was feeling pretty good.

When I was sixteen, I drove my 1964 Chevelle over a small hill. I was taken by ambulance to the hospital and Dr. Bob Hall had to put me to sleep and pull my hip back into place. It took me a little while to get over that one. But a good physician made all the difference.

Years later I would watch this family surgeon remove a section of my father's colon. The old Paintsville hospital, at that time, had a viewing room at one of the surgery rooms. It was quite an experience for a young guy to watch such procedures.

When Jared and Zachary where born, they were delivered by caesarean section. Each time the doctor came in and made the necessary incisions, and out came healthy baby boys. I thought "How wonderful," and I was so grateful for good physicians.

And then for the last eleven years of my life I have visited with this doctor and that doctor, from Lexington, Kentucky to Mayo Clinic in Rochester, Minnesota. Karen and I have sought a physician who might know something that somebody else does not know. Or, who might be willing to try something that nobody else has tried. I know that each of them have in most cases done all they knew to do because there is no known cure for multiple sclerosis.

However, just as Jesus Christ is the greatest preacher of the gospel who ever lived, He was and is the greatest physician of all. Jesus is the Great Physician.

In Mark 5:24–32 we discover Jesus as the Great Physician.

> A large crowd followed and pressed around him. And a woman was there who had been subject to bleeding for twelve years. She had suffered a great deal under the care of many doctors and had spent all she had, yet instead of getting better she grew worse. When she heard about Jesus, she came up behind him in the crowd and touched his cloak, because she

> thought, "If I just touch his clothes, I will be healed." Immediately her bleeding stopped and she felt in her body that she was freed from her suffering.
>
> At once Jesus realized that power had gone out from him. He turned around in the crowd and asked, "Who touched my clothes?"
>
> "You see the people crowding against you," his disciples answered, "and yet you can ask, 'Who touched me?' "
>
> But Jesus kept looking around to see who had done it.

This woman had been sick for 12 years. My wife, Karen, at this writing has been battling MS for 12 years. I think I can relate to the time frame. This was an ongoing illness. She had seen a lot of doctors. She had spent all she had. She was financially broke. She continued to grow worse. She was desperate to get to Jesus and when she touched Him, Jesus felt power leaving His body and this woman was healed of her sickness.

Later in this story Jesus would go to the house of Jairus, where his little girl was apparently in a coma. When Jesus spoke to her, the little girl stood up and walked around the house.

We have heard of occasions were God worked in people's lives to miraculously bring about healing. Often God uses a trained physician.

Time and again some of you have been sick and well and then sick and well. How many times in our lives have we been hurting or sick?

We have been fortunate to overcome the sickness. The body eventually wears out and is no longer able to endure some health problems. We wear our hearts out. Cancer ravages our bodies or age begins to take its toll on us. An incurable disease takes hold of us and destroys our health. And we are grateful that there are good physicians who try to help us.

How are we able to really teach that Jesus is the Great Physician? God let's people get sick, and we die. However, Jesus does for us what nobody else can do. He comforts us like nobody else can.

I was working on my thoughts for a worship service and so I got Karen out of the nursing home where she has had to reside for several months. We were sitting in our car on the parking lot of our church. Our church sits on a beautiful piece of property and provides for a tranquil place to contemplate and pray. I took my Bible out and I said, "Karen, here is a good scripture about how God made the world. And here is one in Jeremiah about how God made man."

She said, "Jeremiah really has a lot of good ones."

I said, "Here is one in Isaiah that I like and I read that to her.

She said, "Yes that would be a good one to read in church." As I read those scriptures to her I sensed God's strength at work in her spirit as well as mine.

Nobody Can Do For the Human Spirit
What Jesus Can Do!

He healed this sick woman of her problem and helped Jairus' daughter to walk, and blind people to see. But He took other lives and gave them a sense of purpose and fulfillment.

Job was having a hard time, but he said in the book of Job chapter 10, verse 12, "You gave me life and showed me kindness and in your providence watched over my spirit."

Psalm 138:3, "When I called, you answered me; you made me bold and stouthearted."

In Daniel 10:18, Daniel gave this testimony, "Again the one who looked like a man touched me and gave me strength. Do not be afraid, O man highly esteemed," he said, "Peace! Be strong now; be strong."

There are great motivators and coaches and teachers, and national and world leaders who inspire us in life, but nobody encourages and inspires us like Jesus does. Are you down today? Cast your cares upon Him because He cares for you. Are you troubled? He will give us rest.

Paul said in Acts 26:22, "But I have had God's help to this very day, and so I stand here and testify to small and great alike."

Nobody Can Treat Your Sin Problem Like Jesus Can

No physician can surgically remove your sin problem. Someone said to me once, "I don't have a cancer problem. I have a sin problem." Then dear friend, you need Dr. Jesus.

Maybe you are thinking at this moment, "I've let unhealthy habits, thoughts, attitudes, arrogance, disobedience, rebellion toward God, and dissension with my brothers in Christ dominate my life and I'm miserable." You need the Great Physician. He is the surgeon general. He is the head chief of staff. He has the antidote that will combat any poison that has entered into your system.

Sin clouds the mind, disrupts our lives, brings misery, makes us depressed, and gives us a feeling of hopelessness. Jesus the Great Physician does for us what no other doctor can do. He goes in and finds the problem and He says, "Here's where the problem is—it's your heart."

Proverbs 14:30, "A heart at peace gives life to the body." That's why David prayed, "Create a pure heart, O God, and renew a steadfast spirit within me." (Psalm 51:10)

How did David's heart get so dirty and messed up? What was wrong with his spirit? Sin. Disobedience to God. How is David's request for cleansing going to happen? John said in 1st John chapter 1:7 "The blood of Jesus, his Son, purifies us from all sin."

David said in Psalm 139:23–24 "Search me, O God, and know my heart; test me and know my anxious thoughts. See if there is any offensive way in me, and lead me in the way everlasting."

Who can help you? A good psychologist? A good psychiatrist? There are times when we all need somebody to talk to but the master of relief is Jesus. You have no other such a friend or brother as you do in the Lord Jesus Christ.

The Bible says, "But God demonstrates his own love for us in this: while we were yet sinners, Christ died for us." (Romans 5:8).

Is sin robbing you of life? Robbing you of happiness? Robbing you of peace?

No One Can Give Direction Like Jesus

What will I do with my life? Whom will I marry? What will be my vocation? Talk to Jesus. Get on your knees and say, "God, I need your direction."

One day a tax collector by the name of Levi was sitting at his tax booth and Jesus said to him, "Follow me." And Levi got up, left everything and followed Jesus Levi held a big party and invited all his lost friends and they complained to Jesus' disciples, "Why do you eat and drink with tax collectors and sinners? And Jesus had an answer for them, He said, "It is not the healthy who need a doctor, but the sick. I have not come to call the righteous, but sinners to repentance." (Luke 5:27–32)

David was just a little shepherd boy. He didn't have a clue about what was in store for him. But God had dramatic plans for the life of David.

Saul was on the Damascus road. He was on a path of hatred to arrest and possibly kill Christians. He was on a road to destruction. But while he was on the Damascus road, Jesus spoke to him . . . "Saul, Saul, why do you persecute me?" Who are you, Lord? Saul asked. And Jesus said, "I am Jesus, whom you are persecuting. Now get up and go into the city, and you will be told what you must do." (Acts 9:4-6)

Never has there been a life more dramatically called out and redirected than Saul who became the great missionary the apostle Paul. God used Paul's life to count and to amount to great things for His sake.

Do you need help in finding your way? Are you treading water? Not sure which way you are going? Lost in life? Lost your way? Are you sort of immobile? Jesus is the Great Physician who can cure your immobility.

I don't like this word immobile because I don't want to be immobile. I want to be on the go. But, I want to know where I'm going. Jesus is the one who says, go, this way. This is the direction. I think that's why Jesus said, "I am the way, and the truth and the life." (John 14:6) He is the way to life.

No One Can Do
For Your Marriage What Jesus Can Do

Do you need a doctor to give you some medicine for your marriage? There are a lot of sick marriages out there, a lot of separation and divorce and people unhappy. A lot of folks saying we need counseling. We need counseling. Friend, they need Dr. Jesus.

I don't hear of marriages where people are praying together and reading the Bible that are falling apart. Doesn't mean you won't have troubles. But Jesus will give your marriage that peace that passes the understanding.

What a wedding day that must have been when Jesus attended that ceremony in Cana and turned the water into wine. That couple would never forget the impact that Jesus had on their wedding and surely on their marriage. In John chapter 2 we have the story how Jesus and His disciples were invited to that wedding. The family was about out of refreshments to serve but Jesus saved the day. He made enough wine to serve everybody and the guests were delighted! Did you invite Jesus to your wedding? If you didn't start out with Jesus, that doesn't mean that it's too late for you to bring God into your home.

Will you say to your husband or wife, "Let's try to do what is right. Let's ask for and invite the help of God into our home." No one can take a good life and make it better like Jesus.

I see people all the time who say life is going so good for me, "I don't need God. I have everything." Friend, He gave it to you. Whether you see it or not, God loans to us everything we have. It is ours briefly. Our spouse. Our jobs. Our kids. This life. Your money. It is yours briefly. The book of James says, "Our lives are like a vapor." We are just momentarily here. But God can take a life that is good and enrich it. Can you imagine your life, if it is already good, being better?

Listen to what David said in Psalm 37:25, "I was young and now I am old, yet I have never seen the righteous forsaken or their children begging bread." I know if you are well and healthy today you don't feel like you need the good doctor Jesus. There is an adage—an ounce of prevention is worth a pound of cure.

God can take your good life and enrich you with His spiritual vitamins. He will lead you to exercise your spirit each day as you refresh yourself in His word and in prayer. He will lead you in the paths of righteousness that will inspire your life and delight your heart!

There's an old hymn we love to sing about the Great Physician: "The great Physician now is near, the sympathizing Jesus; He speaks the drooping heart to cheer, Oh! hear the voice of Jesus. Sweetest note in seraph song, Sweetest name on mortal tongue; Sweetest carol ever sung, Jesus, blessed Jesus. Your many sins are all forgiven, Oh hear the voice of Jesus; Go on your way in peace to heaven, And wear a crown with Jesus."[5]

---

[5] *The Great Physician*, The Baptist Hymnal 188.

CHAPTER SEVENTEEN
REFLECTIONA AND MEDITATION

1. Who is the great physician?

2. How does Jesus minister to the human spirit?

3. How does Jesus treat your sin problems?

4. No one gives direction like Jesus. What is he telling you to do today?

CHAPTER EIGHTEEN

Success Is Getting Up Again!

The story is told of a monk who spent many years of his life in a monastery. One day he was out working in the field and a passerby out of curiosity asked, "Hey, what do you folks do in that monastery all day?" The monk looked up from his work for just a moment and said, "We fall down and we get up. Again he repeated, "We fall down and we get up."

I think this tale is a good story because it captures the spirit of the life who wins. Too many characters to mention in the Bible either fell down or were knocked down. Their tenacity to arise once again inspires us today to greater service.

What would have happened to Joseph had he given up after being sold into slavery? We would not have the inspiring story of his rise to prominence had he quit. What about Paul who was shipwrecked, beaten and imprisoned? Had Paul given up we would not have the inspiring letters of Paul that we have in the Bible. David committed adultery and murdered a man and lost his kingdom. But David got up and went on to be used of God.

Success means getting up. You may fall again. But if you do, you get up again!

Harvey McKay, in his book titled *Pushing the Envelope,* presents a heartwarming list of characters that failed and failed but managed to rise to their feet to experience success.

Abraham Lincoln failed in business, lost numerous elections and his sweetheart, and had a nervous breakdown. But he never quit. He kept trying and became, according to many, our greatest president.

Success means getting up. You may fall again. But if you do, you get up again!

Dr. Seuss's first children's book was rejected by 23 publishers. Michael Jordan was cut from his high school basketball team. Henry Ford failed and went broke five times before he finally succeeded. Franklin D. Roosevelt was struck down by polio but he never quit. Helen Keller, totally deaf and blind, graduated cum laude from Radcliffe College, and went on to become a famous author and lecturer. Adam Clark labored 40 years writing his commentary on the Holy Scriptures.

The History of the Decline and Fall of the Roman Empire took Edward Gibbon 26 painstaking years to complete. Ernest Hemingway is said to have revised The Old Man and the Sea 80 times before submitting it for publication. It took Noah Webster 36 years to compile Webster's Dictionary. The University of Bern rejected Albert Einstein's Ph.D. dissertation, saying it was irrelevant and fanciful.

Johnny Unitas was cut by the Pittsburgh Steelers, but he kept his dream alive by working construction and playing amateur football while staying in contact with every NFL team. The Baltimore Colts finally responded and he became one of the greatest quarterbacks to ever play the game.

Richard Hooker worked seven years on the humorous war novel, M*A*S*H, only to have it rejected by 21 publishers.

Charles Goodyear spent every last dollar over five years filled with experiments to try and develop a rubber life preserver before he succeeded.

A young jockey lost his first, second, third, his first 10, his first 20, and until it became his first 200 and 250 horse races. Finally, Eddie Arcaro won his first race and went on to become one of the great all-time jockeys.

Even Babe Ruth, considered by sports historians to be the greatest baseball player of all time, struck out 1,330 times.

Sir Winston Churchill, himself a person who never quit in a lifetime of defeats and setbacks, delivered the shortest and most eloquent commencement address ever given. Despite taking three years to get through eighth grade because of his trouble learning English grammar, Churchill was asked to address the graduates of Oxford

University. As he approached the podium with his trademark cigar, cane and top hat, he shouted, "Never give up!" Several seconds passed before he rose to his toes and repeated, "Never, never give up." Then he sat down.[6]

What an inspiration to our lives and a delight to our hearts to know that Jesus never gave up. We have a divine Father who never gives up on us. The spirit of success is best seen in those who when at all possible get up after they fall down.

---

[6] Harvey Mackay, Pushing the Envelope: All the Way to the Top (New York: The Ballantine Publishing Group, 1999) 57-59.

CHAPTER EIGHTEEN
REFLECTION AND MEDITATION

1. Have you ever fallen?

2. Who are characters in the Bible who fell but who went on to be used of God?

3. Is it time that you got up from a failure and began life again?

4. God loves you and will never give up on you.

CHAPTER NINETEEN

Stress Relief

Have you ever been stressed? There is a story in the Bible about one of the great Old Testament prophets named Elijah who will provide us some key insights into this problem of stress. Our study scriptures come from 1Kings 19:3 – 8.

Elijah has one of the most dramatic confrontations and victories in the Bible. In this confrontation he faces King Ahab who had abandoned the God of Israel and had followed the worship of Baal. In this scene Elijah calls upon Ahab to bring his false prophets of Baal to Mount Carmel for a demonstration of whose God had the power. Verses 22-24 of chapter 18 say, "Then Elijah said to them, "I am the only one of the Lord's prophets left, but Baal has four hundred and fifty prophets. Get two bulls for us. Let them choose one for themselves, and let them cut it into pieces and put it on the wood but not set fire to it. I will prepare the other bull and put it on the wood but not set fire to it. Then you call on the name of your god, and I will call on the name of the Lord. The god who answers by fire—He is God."

This all had to be a long emotional ordeal for the followers of Baal because the Bible says they called upon the name of Baal from morning till noon. They shouted for Baal to answer them . . . and then they shouted louder and slashed themselves with swords and spears and this lasted until the evening. And the Bible says in verse 29, "no one paid attention."

The Bible then says that Elijah had his sacrifice soaked with water three times and in spite of that "the fire of the Lord fell and burned up the sacrifice, the wood, the stones and the soil, and also licked up the water in the trench." (1 Kings 18:38)

In verse 40, "Then Elijah commanded them, "Seize the prophets of Baal. Don't let anyone get away!" They seized them, and Elijah had them brought down to the Kishon Valley and slaughtered there." This had to be a crazy . . . stressed out, heart wrenching time.

In chapter 19, Ahab tells Jezebel everything Elijah had done and how he had killed all the prophets with the sword. So Jezebel sent a messenger to Elijah to say, "May the gods deal with me, be it ever so severely, if by this time tomorrow I do not make your life like that of one of them." And in verse three of chapter 19 Elijah runs for his life. "When he came to Beersheba in Judah, he left his servant there, while he himself went a day's journey into the desert. He came to a broom tree, sat down under it and prayed that he might die. 'I have had enough, Lord,' he said. 'Take my life; I am no better than my ancestors.' Then he lay down under the tree and fell asleep."

What Is Stress?

Being Too Tired

Often stress means you are too tired. Elijah was exhausted. It had been a long event with the prophets of Baal.

What happens to you when you are flat out drop dead tired? You aren't crisp. You aren't sharp. Let me ask you this question. When you are tired . . . I mean *real* tired . . . do you get cranky? You've worked a long day or you've done a lot of overtime at your job. Or it has taken you a ten hour day to get the house in order and you are exhausted and as soon as you do you have the kids coming in and they're hungry and the husband is wanting to know why supper is late? Or he has had a hard day and he comes home exhausted and stressed out.

Elijah was not only tired but he had been in a long battle. Altogether we are talking about several days of heated battle, even though there had been years of battling leading up to Mount Carmel. Chapter 18 says, "After a long time, in the third year, the word of the Lord came to Elijah: 'Go and present yourself to Ahab, and I will send rain on the land.'"

In verse 16, "Ahab went to meet Elijah. When he saw Elijah, he said to him, "Is that you, you troubler of Israel?" The evil King and the prophet of God had been out of sorts for a long time.

There are all kinds of battles that seem to go on forever. When you are a freshman in high school or a freshman in college you think, "It will never end." And just thinking about it sometimes is stressful.

Transitions Are Tough

You may be new to your area and you think when will this ever start feeling like home or maybe you have to move away and moving of any kind can be a tough transition.

Work may have presented you some tough times of transition. You deal with people who daily present you with challenges and often you have your battles at work. Maybe they've been going on for years. You deal with personality conflicts . . . dissension . . . and it's stressful.

Some of us battle disease and health problems and struggle with the simple issues of life. Disease or disability is a tough transition and it is stressful.

Peer Pressure

Peer Pressure can be intensely stressful. Your boss doesn't like the way you part your hair. Or he seems to be more demanding of you than others in the work place. You have a sales quota thrown on you that Zig Ziglar couldn't obtain. You have deadlines to meet that require day in and day out attention. And the pressure may be getting to you.

Now Elijah had a threat on his life by the queen of Israel. So it was real. And the queen's position of power made it very real to him. Unfortunately, Elijah must have been so tired that he couldn't think very clearly. If God could send fire from heaven and overcome 450 false prophets of Baal, He could surely handle Jezebel. And very soon He would.

Conflict Is a Source of Stress

Conflict may occur within the confines of a long battle, but some things in life are not open battle. They are just sources of differences and disagreements that are never really dealt with or resolved.

It would have been great if Ahab and Jezebel and Elijah could have all found peace in the Lord and their differences resolved. It would have been great if Ahab and Jezebel could have had their hearts changed. But it didn't happen.

Are you in conflict with anyone? We all are different to some extent. All of us need harmony not only within ourselves but we need to live in peace and harmony with other people. And when we don't, that continual conflict is stressful.

Fear Is a Source of Stress

Elijah feared what might happen to him. Life can present challenges and issues that scare us. And fear is stressful.

There is always the fear of what is happening to somebody we love. We wonder, "Is he or she okay?" We fear job loss, security loss, and health loss. We fear the future. We fear what we cannot control.

Stress is too much to do, too many places to be, and far too many perceived expectations.

What is causing stress in your life? (your answer) ______________(don't write this in since you may want to pass this book on to a friend.)

Stress is too much to do, too many places to be, and far too many perceived expectations.

Is it your spouse, family, children, teenagers, lack of money, too many bills, employment conditions, neighbor, or church? Don't ever let church become a place of stress for you. That's not what church is for. Church is not where we go to get stressed out. We go for help, for hope, for love, for friends, for comfort, for direction, for life, to worship Jesus, and to look to the Bible for help.

Negative Results of Stress

One time, this Indian went to see a psychologist for help. He said "Mr. Counselor, sometimes I feel like I'm a wigwam. Other times I feel like a teepee."

And the counselor said, "Oh I know what your problem is, "You're too tense."

Too much stress means too much friction and that leads completely to burn out. You can incinerate in this life and have absolutely nothing left to give. Down in

North Carolina you see these pull off places for run away trucks. Trucks apparently get out of control and they are going so fast that they need a pull off place before they end up in devastation or hurting somebody else. Can you imagine wrecking a 16 wheeler? Can you imagine being hit by one? No fun. And so they have this pulling off place where the truck can steer into and save themselves and save all others in their way.

Sometimes we all may be at that point where we say, "Hey, wait, I'm out of control. I'm pulling off to the side of the road and regaining control before I wreck or hurt somebody."

We hear a lot today about burn out. It's happening everywhere. At work and at home, there are a lot of tired mothers caring for two or three small kids. There are a lot of pressures on Dads and other people where the workload is just killing them.

Too much stress can make you sick. The body and mind can only tolerate so much friction. Stress and worry is like sand in a machine. It wears it out and it shuts it down. Plus, too much stress can make you irritable. It makes you snappy sometimes. Makes you say things you wouldn't normally say.

Positive Results of Stress

A rubber band is useless unless it is under stress. A tea bag is worthless unless it is in hot water. Deadlines can be stressful, but they at least give us a target. Finish lines enable us to have something to run for.

Week in and week out, Sunday is always coming for the minister. Let's imagine a salesman. There are no expectations or deadlines. He has no goals. And most likely he will not be very successful. The student knows the paper is due on a specific date. Finals exams occur on a specific week. Now these may all be stressful to some degree but they at least help us to manage our time and determine what we have to do to accomplish our tasks.

Let's Consider Some Helpful Ideas

Take a break. Jesus took breaks. He got away. In Matthew 14:22-23, "Immediately Jesus made the disciples get into the boat and go on ahead of him to the other side, while he dismissed the crowd. After he had dismissed them, he went up on a mountainside by himself to pray. When evening came, he was there alone."

The story of Elijah is another story of a guy taking a break. Obviously he was under stress but most of the time that's what it takes to push us to do it. This is why we have spring break, fall break, vacation and a day off to recuperate. We are all like Elijah in that sometimes we have to get away. And I think it's noteworthy that he was depressed and didn't feel like living. But that was because for the first time in a long time he stopped, he was alone and had the opportunity to think. According to the scripture he rested, he ate a good meal and rejuvenated himself. And then he moved on.

Jesus turned to the Father. When Jesus obviously was stressed out about what was going to happen to Him on the cross, He went into the garden of Gethsemane to pray. He knew if He ever needed the Father it was then. That's why the scene of His death on the cross is one of such agony. He dies completely alone without the help of the Father. When He was with His inner circle of disciples on the Mt. of Transfiguration He was talking with the heavenly Father. Jesus knew it was vitally important to stay in communication with the Father.

Ask For Help

Jesus said, "Ask, and it shall be given you," (Matthew 7:7). What is causing your stress? If it's financial, see someone who has some ability in that field to help you. It may be a banker or it may be an attorney or a trusted friend.

If your problem is school related, talk to the teachers. Or, if it is a medical condition, talk to a doctor. Your problem may require an attorney.

If your level of stress is *too much to do,* talk to a close friend or family member and say, "I'm overloaded with too much to do. What do you think?"

Always talk to the Father. He is always available. There are wise and godly people who are available to pray with you and who will try to provide some guidance.

I wonder how many of our spiritual or emotional problems might be solved by simply taking them seriously and contemplatively . . . to the Lord and just being honest and forthright with God.

There are some things your parents, your friends, and others can help you with. There are some stresses where only God can help you. Only God can forgive you of your sins. Only God can give you power to survive and work through many of your greatest problems.

With God all things are possible!

A young man on the verge of dying from a very negative lifestyle told me while he was figuratively hanging by the last thread of his rope, "I'm not going to make it." I said, "With God all things are possible. With God's help you can make it and work through these negative destructive factors that are tearing you down." With God's help he began to slowly recuperate and build back his life, and now he is a testimony of God's power and help.

What a beautiful thought for your day! This is a wonderful way for you to begin or even end your day knowing that whatever you are facing, "With God all things are possible!" Delight yourself in this good and delicious thought! Be encouraged in your heart and spirit that God is an awesome God and life is too short to go around beaten down and all stressed out!

CHAPTER NINETEEN
REFLECTION AND MEDITATION

1. What caused Elijah stress?

2. What causes you stress?

3. How did Elijah overcome his stress?

4. What is stress?

5. What are some helpful ways to manage stress?

CHAPTER TWENTY

Second Chances

"And when you stand praying, if you hold anything against anyone, forgive him, so that your Father in heaven may forgive you your sins." (Mark 11:25)

Luke 6:36, "Be Merciful, just as your Father is merciful."

Luke 17:3-4, "So watch yourselves. If your brother sins, rebuke him, and if he repents, forgive him. If he sins against you seven times in a day, and seven times comes back to you and says, I repent, forgive him."

I think we all at least one time in our lives have thought we deserved a second chance. You may have misunderstood an assignment in school and did your best but when you turned it in you discovered that it was done wrong. And you may have gone to the teacher and said, "I thought you said to do such and such."

But the teacher said, "No, I meant this."

And you said, "Oh no, then it's all wrong and I'm going to get a zero. Would you give me a chance to do it over?" And depending on your teacher you may or may not get another chance. But you are grateful if you do, so that you might do it right and receive the passing grade.

Have you ever been pulled over by a policeman and he checked your driver's license, looked at your registration and then he came back and said, "This is just a warning, slow down and have a good day." And you breathed a sigh of relief because he had shown some mercy on you. You felt like you had been given a second chance.

My father has been blessed in years past. He had colon cancer but survived it. He had both breast muscles removed and survived that. And then he survived an aneurysm in his aorta.

Very likely you have known all kinds of second chances in life. Maybe you were close to divorce. And you sought help and decided you would give your marriage another chance.

Sometimes we get frustrated with people at work and church but if we want to do the right thing, we give people a second chance.

Have you ever washed your hands of something or somebody and said, "I just can't go any farther with that person. I have tried and tried and I can't do it any more. I can no longer survive the pain of loving that person, tolerating that person or enduring that situation."

It may be an abusive spouse that has beaten you for the last time and you've said that's it, "I'm out of here." It may be a child. You've tried, wept, loved and spent until you are unable to do it any more and you've said,

"That's it I can't go another mile with this child. I'm done." That's a painful decision.

Or it may be a job and you've said, "I'm going to try to please my boss for three more months and if I can't get one good word for my efforts then I'm done." Sometimes in life we get second chances. Sometimes we give them and sometimes we don't.

People who murder and commit acts of violence that take the life of another cold heartedly, seldom get second chances from juries to roam the streets again—and well they shouldn't.

We've seen car crashes where there was maybe just a slight judgment in error but it cost a loss of life and there was no chance to change the error and bring those people back from life.

In an east Kentucky county back in the sixties, a bus driver drove a busload of kids into the Big Sandy River. None of those children or the bus driver escaped. The pastor of a local church said that for over two weeks there would be one call after another saying, "We've found another child in the river please come and go with us." Not one of those children had a chance to escape that bus, nor did they even get a second chance to start the day over. None of them had the chance to say, "Wait this day is not turning out so good. Let's get off this bus and start this day over again." They didn't get that chance. You do not always get a second chance.

In the Old Testament Aaron's two sons Nadab and Abihu were disobedient and God struck them dead. Moses never got to enter the land of promise.

We only have one life and we have many opportunities and many chances. But we all hear people say, "If I could live my life over, or if I could raise my kids again, or do my marriage over . . . do school over." But we just have one life.

In the New Testament there is a story in Luke 16 about a man who asked for another chance, but life was over.

Second Chances often come after a period of hardship and great expense. Jonah is an Old Testament story about a man that was asked to do something by God. He ran from God and even thought he was successfully hiding. In a short time, he was swallowed by a fish. He was allowed to live and only after this painful experience did he receive a second chance.

> *Second Chances often come after a period of hardship and great expense.*

Moses murdered an Egyptian and it cost him 40 years in the wilderness. David and Bathsheba sinned against God and they lost their little boy in death. It was such a trying time in the palace. His disobedience cost him.

Paul had lived a life as a persecutor of Christians and even after his conversion he had to prove himself to be real. That had to be difficult for Paul constantly trying to communicate to others that his Christianity was for real.

People are reluctant about second chances. Your pet dog may give you a second chance. You can talk bad to your dog, scold him and he'll come back wagging his tail. However, people in general are reluctant at second chances.

People say, "Oh I remember what you said. Or, I remember how you stole from me. I remember how you did me." The word gets around. "Did you remember what he did 5 years ago? Ten years ago?" People remember.

Is there any place that a man, woman, boy or girl can go and get a second chance? Has anybody ever given you a second chance?

God is the God of a second chance. How many chances do we need in life, one? I've found that the average person in life needs a second chance, a third, a fourth, a fifth, a sixth, a hundred and more. You know why? We mess up so much. We mess up because we are so human. Mankind has been messing up since Adam and Eve.

> *We mess up because we are so human.*

How about you? Have you ever messed up in life? Possibly you have time and time again. We want second chances. But do we *give* them freely? Matthew 18:21–35 has a story about a guy who wanted a second chance and he received it. And then he turned right around and had a fellow beg him for a second chance to pay a debt. This forgiven man had him thrown into prison until he could pay the debt. But some people found out about him and told the man who had forgiven him. This man had him brought in and said, "Shouldn't you have had mercy on your fellow servant just as I had on you? In anger his master turned him over to the jailers to be tortured, until he should pay back all he owed. Verse 35, "This is how my heavenly Father will treat each of you unless you forgive your brother from your heart." Have you been forgiven? God says we are to forgive others.

The ministry of Jesus Christ was a ministry of second chances. Now He told the woman caught in sin, "Then neither do I condemn you, go now and leave your life of sin." Do you think she never sinned again? Maybe not the way she was caught in sin, but in some way she likely made other mistakes and committed other sins.

Jesus was asked, "Lord, how many times shall I forgive my brother when he sins against me? Up to seven times?" Jesus answered, "I tell you, not seven times, but seventy-seven times." (Matthew 18:21-22)

Peter was humiliated after denying he even knew Jesus three times. He wept over his failure. But Jesus said to him as many times as Peter denied Him to go back to work feeding His sheep for Him. Peter a little later would address thousands of people on the day of Pentecost and thousands made life-changing decisions for Christ.

Here is a threefold principle:

1. **Mess up.**
2. **Clean up.**
3. **Be used of God.**

It happened with Jonah. It happened with John Mark in the New Testament. It happened with Peter. The New Testament book of 1st John 1:9 says, "If we confess our sins, he is faithful and just to forgive us our sins and purify us from all unrighteousness."

Second Chances Are Based On Attitude

Jesus talked about a Publican and the Pharisee. The Pharisee was far too arrogant and self-righteous. The publican smote his chest and said, "God be merciful to me a sinner." The prodigal son in Luke chapter 15 had lost everything while living in a far away country. Life had become so difficult for him. With an attitude of humility he came home to ask his father's help. He never even had to ask. The father saw him coming from a distance and ran out to meet him.

Second Chances Are Based On Admission

The prodigal son had determined within his heart that he was going to say to his father that he had sinned and messed up in life.

Zacchaeus was a man that had taken too much money from people as a tax collector in the day of Jesus. One day Jesus ate dinner with him and Zacchaeus said that he would repay those he had stolen from fourfold.

Second Chances Are Based On Action

This means saying, "I messed up and want to be used again." The prodigal son did not spend the rest of his life wallowing around saying, "I've sinned. I'm bad, my life is over." That's why Jesus was saying, yes Peter you made a horrible mistake, but get with it and feed my sheep.

Every Sunday we have all kinds of people who go to church. Adulterers, liars, thieves, murderers, people who have had abortions, people who fear they have HIV, people who have lost a lot financially or lost their jobs, people who have lost a husband or wife, lost a child, messed up in marriage, and messed up in life. What should be done with these people?

If they want a second chance then we should give them one. And maybe a third and a fourth chance. God has given all of us so many chances. If they want to serve, we give them opportunities to serve. God used Peter and John Mark and adulterous people and murderers like Paul. Who would we be to say, "You messed up one time and we can't use you."

What will happen to us when we give second chances? We will be blessed. Jesus said, "For if you forgive men when they sin against you, your heavenly father will also forgive you." (Matthew 6:14)

If we want forgiveness, hope and mercy, then we have to offer it. And when we do, we will be blessed. The good, delightful, wonderful grace and love of Jesus

Christ now is being offered to those who would like a second chance. Do you want one? Do you need one? Would you like to be forgiven of your sins? Do you want a new and fresh start in life? Do you want to begin your life again? The good news is that *you can.*

2 Corinthians 5:17 says, "Therefore, if anyone is in Christ, he is a new creation; the old has gone, the new has come!"

CHAPTER TWENTY
REFLECTION AND MEDITATION

1. Have you ever needed a second chance?

2. Do you need to give someone a second chance?

3. Has God ever given you a second chance?

4. We have a wonderful God of second chances. Thank Him at this moment for His forgiveness and love.

CHAPTER TWENTY-ONE

Don't Give Up

Dealing with Discouragement

What does it take to discourage you?

You fill out your tax report and you have itemized everything possible and you discover you owe $3,000. And you think, "That's a back breaker."

You go to the mailbox and your utility bill is astronomical. A friend of mine said their heating bill was over $500 last month and she couldn't believe it.

Maybe you spend all day cleaning the house and finally it seemed you had it altogether and then the next day you couldn't tell it had ever been touched. It looked like a cyclone had gone through your house.

Or, maybe the place you have your car serviced said, "It's your transmission it will cost you $1,900 to replace it."

Discouragement may come to you when you have begged, pleaded and prayed for your kids to work a little harder on the books at school and then the report card shows they didn't. And you wonder, "Is there any use?"

You may have gone through this in a lot of different ways in life. You may have become discouraged in your marriage. Marriage wasn't what you thought it was going to be or the person you married wasn't who you thought she/he was and so you soon became discouraged. Or maybe a scenario or situation developed in your marriage that you had not counted on and it became horribly frustrating for you to daily cope with all that you had to handle, and discouragement took over.

I talked to a man the other day that has been at his job for 20 years. He said, "They have been great to me, but lately they have just piled it on me and made my life miserable. I'm really discouraged."

Maybe you've been caught in a company downsize and lost your job. Or maybe there is the rumor that your company is cutting back and it's more than discouraging . . . it's scary.

Discouragement Comes In Different Forms

There is the cancer patient that is fighting the deadly disease with all his fiber. It's chemo every week, but the oncologist says, "We've found cancer in another part of your body." He doesn't come out and tell you that you are losing the battle but you know you are and discouragement sets in.

Maybe you are a student and you grapple every day with Algebra or Spanish . . . and you are behind in your class. Your schoolmates seem to understand the work but you aren't getting it and you are really discouraged in your studies.

Or maybe you are discouraged about a friendship or relationship. It could be somebody at work. You've tried to be congenial, helpful and professional, but this person you have to work with is driving you crazy and it's discouraging. It may be a fellow church member. You've gone out of your way to be nice, cordial, and speak. You have tried to work with this person but they are impossible. And this person may think you are impossible and so you are really frustrated about it and discouraged.

Pressure to succeed can get to us and discourage us. The boss may apply pressure. Church leadership may apply pressure on ministerial leadership to succeed. Or the school administration conveys to the coach that he must have a winning season or his job is over. Pressure makes us do one of two things:

1. We work really hard to succeed.
2. We get discouraged

And when you are doing your best, praying, planning and begging people to work with you in whatever you are trying to accomplish; knowing that there is some expectation to be successful, and the people who expect you to be successful don't help you, then it's discouraging.

The devil is wise. In the Garden of Eden, he is the slithering serpent. In the Old Testament book of Job, he is the unseen force of destruction. In the wilderness he pulls out all the stops to bringing down the Son of God as he stoops to all levels to discourage and tempt even Jesus Christ.

What Else May Bring About Discouragement?

We get discouraged when we are tired. Are you tired today? Do you feel bad? Discouraged? Maybe it's because you are exhausted? Take a break. Rest. You aren't a machine. Machines can be replaced. Good people can't. Take care of yourself physically and emotionally. Most of us don't have anybody standing guard over us demanding that we take time to rest and replenish ourselves. In the Old Testament book of Kings, I think Elijah was discouraged because he was so exhausted after his battle with the false prophets of Baal. After he rested and ate a meal he felt better. You always think and react better after a little rest.

We get discouraged when the demands are greater than our ability to respond. The disciples couldn't cast out a demon. "Why couldn't we drive it out?" (Matthew 17:19) There are those times in life when the requirement upon us is more than we can give. And we find ourselves not being able to overcome or arise to the challenge, and it is discouraging.

We get discouraged when people let us down. In the New Testament Paul was excited about John Mark's travel with him on a missionary journey. But when John Mark got home sick, it irritated Paul a little because he thought John Mark was letting them down. Do you set your sights on people and they mess up and you feel discouraged by it? That's why our eyes should always be on Jesus. He is the author and finisher of our faith.

We get discouraged when life isn't going the way we had planned or had hoped. The disciples on the road to Emmaus said, "We had hoped." (Luke 24:21) When Jesus was crucified their hopes were shattered.

What would make a high school teenager in California carry a pistol to school and take the lives of other classmates? One such incident was reported in Southern California of one such student. He was so down and discouraged by how he had been treated by other classmates. They had made fun of his appearance. He felt alone and isolated. In his mind he felt that it was his only way to deal with the discouraging situation. Of course he was very wrong and needed emotional and spiritual help. But how many people are so discouraged to the point that they are literally tormented to destruction?

> *If you can't find anything else to do in life, then find a way to be a ray of sunshine and a model of encouragement.*

One special point at this juncture of this chapter:

Do your best whenever possible to help others. And there is no better way to help others than through encouragement. Find a way to encourage others. Jesus is our model of encouragement. Barnabas was the disciple of encouragement. If you can't find anything else to do in life, then find a way to be a ray of sunshine and a model of encouragement. I guarantee you that you will have a tremendous opportunity of service.

When You Are Discouraged, There Are Ways To React

Don't get crazy. Killing someone is not the way. Just running off and leaving town is not another. Hurting someone verbally is not a way to react to discouragement. People never forget words.

Talk to somebody and say, "I'm really discouraged can you help me?" Maybe they can or can't but it helps sometimes to verbalize it.

Pray with somebody. Is there anybody in the world that you feel will pray with you? Every person should cultivate a spiritual friendship with someone with whom to pray.

Take a break. Remove yourself from whatever is discouraging you for a few days or even a couple of weeks and see how you feel about it. After a break, sometimes even a few days away gives us a chance to have a different perspective.

Try another angle. Sometimes we try the same methods over and over again to win a battle or resolve a situation. Some methods are not always fail proof and what worked at one time may not work another. Be open to dealing with your discouragement in a different way.

Do your best to deal with it. This can be much easier said than done. And our ability to cope with certain circumstances may have a breaking point. That's why the next point is very vitally important.

Give it to God. Talk to God about your discouragement. Bring your defeats, concerns, ambitions, stresses and any problem that you have to our wonderful Lord. The Bible tells us time and again about how much He loves us. God will help you and see you through whatever you are dealing with in your life. Like all the other great people of God in the Bible, you will face discouragements and hardships just like they did. Sometimes you will fail, like all humans do. But, we have a great and mighty God who helps us through our pain and discouraging times. He is there for you to call upon in prayer because He cares for you.

CHAPTER TWENTY-ONE
REFLECTION AND MEDITATION

1. What does it take to discourage you?

2. What are some causes of discouragement?

3. When discouraged there are ways to react.

4. There are seven ways to react. What are the seven reactions to discouragement?

Also by Dr. Glenn Mollette

Silent Struggler

A Caregiver's Personal Story

This book is the personal story of Glenn Mollette and his role as caregiver to his wife, Karen. Silent Struggler deals with almost every issue faced by the caregiver. This is a must book for every family or person experiencing chronic illness in a care-giving role.

Silent Struggler can be ordered through your local bookstore or the Internet. Check out Amazon.com, barnesandnoble.com, BooksaMillion.com or Borders.com.

ISBN 0-9704650-0-9
Published by Inspiration.

Printed in the United States
830000003B

9 780970 465023